Outnumbered,
Not Outsmarted!

Outnumbered, *Not* Outsmarted!

An A to Z Guide for Working with Kids and Teens in Groups

Cathi Cohen, LCSW

Dedication

My work has been inspired by the experiences, ideas, and day-to-day interactions with the many children in my life, and it is to them that I dedicate this book: my wonderful kids Jesse, Dov, and Lyana; my nephews and niece Matthew, Benjamin, Daniel, Jonathan, Alex, and Jennifer; and the hundreds of children from the Stepping Stones social skills groups since 1995.

ISBN13: 978-0-9714609-4-2

ISBN10: 0-9714609-4-9

Published by

ADVANTAGE BOOKS

3268 Arcadia Place, N.W.

Washington, DC 20015

Cover and graphics by Barbara Michaluk

The material presented in this book is based solely on the experience of the author and is intended for informational purposes only. This book is not meant as a substitute for medical or psychological advice or treatment and should not be construed as such. Stories contained in this book are not based on actual persons except where specified.

For more information about our books, including information on bulk discounts, Please write to us, call 888-238-8588 (toll free), or visit our website at

www.advantagebooks.net

Manufactured in the United States of America

10 9 8 7 6 5 4 3 2 1

ADVANTAGE BOOKS

Washington, DC 20015

Table of Contents

Introduction

Even the most experienced and enthusiastic of adult leaders are flummoxed by some of the dynamics and behaviors that crop up when working with kids in groups. One-on-one, most kids are an absolute delight. Get them together in groups, and it's a whole different matter!

Whether you are a teacher, a camp counselor, a Girl or Boy Scout leader, or a soccer coach, you know when your kids are getting the most

out of your group. The group environment is a peaceful one, and you feel confident and secure that your kids are getting along and working cooperatively to achieve common goals. Your group members participate and support each other. Their enthusiasm and positive energy is contagious and self-sustaining. Working with these kids makes you feel like you are a terrific leader and can handle any issues that might come up. If the team you are coaching shows poor sportsmanship, you know how to handle it. If the students you are teaching are unruly, you know how to turn the negative behavior into positive. When the campers in your bunk fight with each other, you know how to help them resolve it.

But, let's be real. Even the most talented of you are tested from time to time. You may be comfortable with discipline, but not know how to build cooperation. You may be a master at handling bullying, but when a child asks you a personal question, you are tongue tied. Working with kids may not be difficult for you, but working with their parents? That's a different story altogether!

As a licensed clinical social worker and certified group psychotherapist, I've been counseling children in social skills training groups since fore that. It became clear early on in my work with kids that they behave very differently one-on-one than they do in groups. Children who appeared confident, warm, and carefree in my office behaved very differently in groups with other kids. These kids expressed to me privately how frustrated and saddened they were at their schools, in their neighborhoods, and at their social activities because they didn't fit in. *Stepping Stones*, our social skills training program, grew out of a desperate need for kids to learn the skills necessary to make and keep friends. They could only do this in groups with other kids where they could see themselves through others' eyes. There is a distinct social complexity in groups that does not exist in a one-on-one setting. Groups are a natural setting for kids to form alliances, test boundaries, and push their own emotional limits.

The primary goal of our *Stepping Stones* groups is to help the socially challenged child develop positive peer relationships. We are able to use to our benefit the natural interpersonal dynamics that arise any time there are more than three children in a room. When conflicts come up, we encourage the use of negotiating and compromising skills. When new children join one of our groups, we help our kids with welcoming and joining-in skills. When the kids get angry with each other, we help them express their anger in appropriate ways. Our groups offer ongoing opportunities for children to learn and grow.

I've observed over the years that the complex interactions our *Stepping Stones* leaders handle in our therapy groups are no different from the dynamics that occur on my daughter's soccer field or in my son's bunk at summer camp. The leadership challenges exist regardless of the focus or structure of the group. Children exhibit common patterns of behavior when they are together. You have a mission as their leader to use your knowledge and experience to promote both individual and group growth. To be the most effective leader you can be, you'll want to have the necessary tools to manage any problem you face in your group. From this book, you'll learn strategies and techniques to deal with the typical challenges of working with groups of children.

How to Use This Book

You have picked up *Outnumbered, Not Outsmarted!* because you are a caring adult who wants to learn how to work with a group of children more effectively. You may be struggling with an issue that is specific to one child or with a dynamic that is impacting the entire group. In an A-Z format, this book highlights many of the major interpersonal challenges that develop in groups of kids. Each chapter offers concrete steps you can take to understand and address the issue, as well as specific things you can say when you are at a loss for words. You will be asked to try and practice new strategies when you are working with your kids. Some of these techniques will feel natural and comfortable to you. Others will not. Do what feels right for you and your leadership style, and at the same time, work outside your comfort zone. Challenge yourself to try new ways of relating to your group members.

You don't need to read the book chronologically, from start to finish. Feel free to focus as much energy and time necessary on the areas where you need the most help. Take a look at the table of contents. See which of the chapters speak most personally to you. Keep the book next to your bed. Pick it up and refer to it often. Be patient with yourself when you find yourself falling into old patterns of behavior that have not been successful in the past. We tend to get into a groove as leaders, even when those grooves aren't working for us.

Learning new leadership skills is hard and requires practice. Take it slowly, one step at a time. Good luck!

Anger
Taming the Tiger Within

Anger is a natural emotion, but a complicated one. For kids and adults alike, anger often comes at a cost. Gone unchecked, anger can hurt others and damage relationships. Expressing anger productively may take years to develop. And, for some, may never happen. Expecting a group of kids to never lose their cool is like expecting snow in the Bahamas!

Handling a Child's Anger

Thirteen-year-old Lisa is a very talented basketball guard. A strong shooter, Lisa consistently leads her team in points. She is fast and confident on the court. Her coach claims he hasn't seen such a strong seventh grade player in years. However, Lisa has one problem on the court. She has a temper. During their last game, a player on the opposing team elbowed Lisa to get to the ball. Lisa responded by shoving her so hard, her opponent fell and hurt her arm. The referees removed Lisa from the game and her team went on to lose.

Lisa's coach had a private talk with Lisa after the game. Together, they identified some of Lisa's anger buttons and a strategy for channeling her anger into competitive play.

1

Anger is a normal, healthy emotion that all kids feel from time to time. In fact, it can actually be a helpful emotion because it's a signal that something is wrong and needs to change. As kids learn to feel more comfortable with anger and expressing it in a controlled fashion, they can begin to appreciate its benefits.

Anger becomes destructive when there is too much of it, or it is expressed inappropriately – in either an uncontrolled (as in Lisa's case) or an over-controlled manner. How can a child "over-control" her anger, you might ask? Isn't that a good thing? Unfortunately, the longer a child sits on a lot of anger without verbalizing it, the more likely it is that she will blow her top. Over-controlled kids are like powder kegs waiting to explode.

The first step in helping kids manage their anger is helping them to understand its roots and how the body exhibits anger. Then you can move on to helping kids express anger appropriately.

① Let the child know you understand anger.

First and foremost, kids need to know that it's okay to feel angry. You need to help them understand the difference between "the feeling" and "the action." Lisa's feelings toward her opponent may have been appropriate; however, shoving her was not. Her coach didn't need to tell Lisa that her behavior was unacceptable. The referee made that very clear when he removed her from the game. Instead, the coach helped diffuse Lisa's anger by focusing on how she could manage it. He helped her understand that anger is a common emotion that all players experience, and that there are opportunities to constructively channel her anger into the game, thereby enabling her to become a better competitor. Her coach might have said, "I can see why that player made you angry, Lisa, but you know that you can't express your anger by shoving your opponent. Next time you get mad on the court, try showing it by playing better in the game."

There are many ways that you can let your kids know that you understand their anger. This doesn't mean that you are encouraging unacceptable expressions of anger.

Try Saying This:

"Ronnie, I know you get really mad when you lose a match, but I still can't let you throw your racquet."

"Mona, you've made it clear to us that you do not appreciate being teased, even in jest. How can you let us know you are hurt without screaming?"

"I can see that you are angry with Kyle for getting you in trouble. Let's think of a way to tell him with words, not actions."

You might need to discuss and define for your group the line between unacceptable and acceptable expressions of anger. Kids are certainly aware that hitting, kicking, and pushing are off limits. But they may be less aware that name calling, back stabbing, and screaming are also unacceptable expressions of anger. Give some thought to what you consider positive expressions of anger and communicate them to your group. Directing anger into game play or the use of "I feel..." statements to communicate feelings are two ways to express anger acceptably. Encourage your kids to voice what they think constitutes positive expressions of anger.

Expressing Anger

Acceptable Ways:	Unacceptable Ways:
▶ Using words	▶ Using our hands or feet
▶ Telling the person we are angry with them one-on-one	▶ Gossiping
▶ Writing down our angry feelings	▶ Using sarcasm
▶ Punching a punching bag	▶ Backstabbing

2　Help the child discover what "pushes her buttons" (makes her angry).

The first step in gaining control over anger is learning which situations trigger anger. Ask the kids to tell you what pushes their buttons. Once they are more self-aware, kids are able to:

▸ Avoid situations that will anger them

▸ Come up with solutions to deal with their anger ahead of time

▸ Soothe themselves when confronted with an anger-producing event

---

Common Button Pushers for Kids

▸ Not getting what they want

▸ Losing a game

▸ Getting teased

▸ Being mocked (provoked)

▸ When things "aren't fair"

▸ Other kids telling them what to do

▸ Tattletaling

3　Recognize the warning signs.

It's especially difficult for kids to reign themselves in once they've become angry. If you know your group very well, you can begin to identify each individual's early warning signs. Once you're aware of the signals, you can intervene *before* it's too late, and the child has lost it. Kids with anger issues need help tuning into their bodies to notice their own early warning signs. Here are some common ones you will observe in your kids:

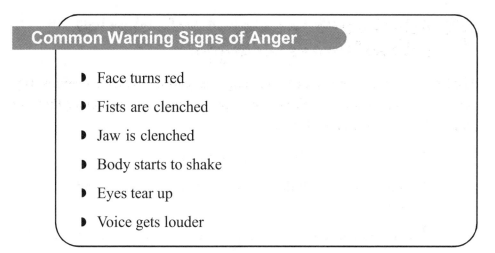

Common Warning Signs of Anger

- ▶ Face turns red
- ▶ Fists are clenched
- ▶ Jaw is clenched
- ▶ Body starts to shake
- ▶ Eyes tear up
- ▶ Voice gets louder

In Lisa's case, the coach knew that when Lisa was getting angry, her face changed from a determined look to a scowl. She also bit her tongue. When these warning signs occurred, the coach and Lisa developed a code word to help her pull herself together. The word was "red." Only Lisa and her coach knew the code word. The plan was for Lisa to take a deep breath and relax when she heard the word. If she was unable to relax her face, she knew that the coach would pull her off the court to give her time to cool down and regroup.

The coach uses a code word to distract Lisa away from her anger and help her disengage from what's provoking her. In this way, the coach intervenes *before* Lisa's "point of no return" (before she acts aggressively). By following this plan, he helps her monitor her own feelings so that she has the chance to choose a different path of expression for her anger.

Tune in to your kids' warning signs. They may have trouble knowing when their own anger is escalating. You may see it before they do. When you do, figure out your own special way to let them know they are getting angry and need to cool off. You may choose a code word like Lisa's coach, or use a hand signal like I did with Nico.

Nico was an eleven-year-old boy enrolled in our *Stepping Stones* outdoor summer program. As much as Nico enjoyed the games and exercises we played in the group, he struggled with his anger when he perceived the group's rules to be "unfair." Nico would let us know he was angry by yelling, crying, and ultimately refusing to play with the rest of the group. All were unacceptable ways to deal with his anger. As soon as we noticed that Nico grit his teeth *prior* to an angry outburst, we were able to help him cool down before he lost control. Nico and I developed a signal. When I pulled my right ear lobe, he knew that I was telling him I noticed him clenching his teeth and he needed to cool down. In this way, we helped Nico disconnect from his anger before he exploded.

4 Develop a plan-of-action with the child.

Now that the child has a better idea of what makes her angry, you can begin to help her express anger differently. It's not enough to tell a kid that her behavior is unacceptable. She needs to learn and practice skills to replace old ways of managing anger.

Coping Strategies for Kids

- Take a self-imposed time-out.

- Distance myself from the person or thing that's pushing my buttons.

- Focus on the task at hand.

- Tell a friend how I'm feeling.

- Tell myself "Everything is okay."

- Take a deep breath.

- Think it through before I react.

In Lisa's case, she and the coach decided that Lisa could ask to be put on the bench if she was feeling like she might become physically aggressive. Knowing that she had the option to take a self-imposed time-out helped Lisa to gain control. In time, she rarely got to the point where she needed to be pulled from the game.

⑤ Praise effort, not just results.

Actively chart the progress of the child's movement toward her goal of anger control. If you notice an improvement, write it down so that you won't forget to communicate it.

Be on the constant lookout for the little victories. Gaining control over anger is a long-term process that won't be achieved overnight. Along the way, offer the child praise for effort, not just results. Praising them in front of the entire group is a powerful way to reward their progress and keep them motivated to continue learning to manage their anger.

Reminder

**Praise in a group;
criticize in private!**

As an adult leader, you communicate to your kids at all times that you have confidence in them and their ability to make changes as a group and as individuals. It's up to you to highlight progress even when the going gets tough. Anger control is one of the toughest skills to develop. The more you communicate your confidence in someone's ability to manage their anger effectively, the better they'll get at it.

Bullying
Coping with Meanness

Jack's first summer at month-long sleep away camp was difficult. He loved all of the activities, especially tennis, archery, and theatre. He thought he had the best counselors in the camp. He even had a friend named Will in his bunk who he knew from home. But Jack complained of one problem – a couple of the boys in the bunk were mean to him. He didn't really understand what they had against him. They called him names, wouldn't sit near him at lunch, and sometimes tripped him when he walked by. Will tried to help Jack by telling him what he observed. He said that the boys didn't like Jack because he constantly annoyed them by "getting in their faces," even when they asked him to stop. Will suggested that Jack back off and stop bugging the boys. Jack didn't like Will's advice. He preferred to see himself as a victim of the boys' bullying, which continued for the rest of the summer. The counselors didn't seem to notice what was going on, or they thought that Jack deserved his fate, or they just assumed "boys will be boys; they'll work it out." When Jack left camp at the end of the summer, he told his parents that he didn't want to ever go back. Jack's parents were upset that he was bullied. They mailed complaint letters to the camp, and never again sent Jack to sleep away camp.

Bullying is one of the most painful experiences of childhood. Whether a child is bullied or is doing the bullying, either way he may suffer long-lasting consequences. This chapter will help you manage bullying more effectively. As an adult who works with kids, you're committed to their safety and well-being. An essential step in ensuring your group's emotional and physical safety is setting the stage properly so that bullying doesn't occur. By maintaining a proactive stance against bullying, you lead the way for the kids to treat each other with respect.

Sometimes, regardless of your best efforts to prevent it, bullying will occur. In this case, it is important that you:

- know the difference between good-natured teasing and bullying;

- familiarize yourself with the signs of bullying;

- differentiate between male and female bullying;

- learn how to help the bully as well as the bullied.

What is Bullying?

Bullying is described as one or more individuals causing physical or emotional harm to another. It is the *repeated exposure* over time to threatening actions that makes it different from the benign teasing most kids experience in childhood. Benign teasing is usually a short-term situation – perhaps a verbal putdown, or a negative whisper or comment by one individual toward another. Bullying is an escalation of teasing into a regular pattern that can occur over a period of days, weeks, even months.

Girls and Boys Do Not Bully the Same

Girls and boys are equally likely to be bullied. But the way boys and girls bully is quite different. Girls who are constantly teased or bullied become socially ostracized. Rather than launch a head-on assault like boys do, girls tend to tease indirectly. A female ringleader will whisper behind a girl's back rather than call her names or physically confront her. The ringleader will make sure that no one invites a particular girl to a party, for instance. A female victim might find mean notes in her desk or hear false gossip being spread about her. Girls make it very clear who is "in" and who is "out." Because of the indirect nature of female bullying, it can be tricky to reckon with, both for adults and for kids who see it and are afraid to speak out. When confronted, the girls who engage in this type of bullying can easily deny that it's even taking place.

Boys, on the other hand, tend to be more straightforward in their bullying. They use more blunt methods – name calling, mimicking, and physical threats. Boys push, trip (as in Jack's case), threaten, and harass one another.

The experience of being bullied is painful. The worst teasing among girls typically occurs in elementary school and begins to die down in middle school. Boys do a majority of their bullying in middle school. If you lead a group of high schoolers, you may notice that bullying has dissipated, but be on the lookout for social alienation at this stage. Teenagers who were bullied in elementary and/or middle school may say that they feel "invisible." These socially isolated teenagers are at risk for depression, loneliness, and suicide in adulthood.

Setting the Stage to Prevent Bullying

1 Create a positive environment.

Being upbeat and positive is contagious! The kids look to you to set the tone for the group. Whether you're a teacher, a coach, or a camp counselor, you, as the primary role model, must remain relentlessly inspirational. Not a simple task. When things go wrong, it can be difficult to remain encouraging. As adults, our impulse is to try to regain control through negative words or punishment. I encourage you to do all that you can to maintain a positive, constructive tone for your group. Help the group maintain this tone by verbally reinforcing appropriate social behaviors in *all* group members.

"You've done a great job cleaning up together!"

"What a team! You guys work so well together!"

"We have a great team because you take care of each other!"

"Hey, guys, thanks for getting together to work on that skill. I see great improvement!"

Treating colleagues, parents, and above all, the kids with respect and thoughtfulness goes a long way in maintaining a healthy environment for children.

② Set rules of conduct up front.

Whether you run a classroom, coach a team, or lead a bunk, it's important to establish and enforce rules at the beginning of your time together. It's much easier to loosen up on the rules as you go along than it is to tighten up. If it's possible, allow your kids to set their own rules. They'll get great experience learning how to manage their own behaviors.

Establishing Rules Up Front

▶ Help the group to establish its tone. "What kind of group do you want to have?" "Are there behaviors that are unacceptable for this group?" "How about bullying?" "What should you do if you notice someone is being bullied?"

▶ Ask the kids to set up their own rules. When kids work together to come up with their own rules, they're more likely to follow them.

▶ Write the rules down.

Establishing Rules Up Front (cont'd)

> ▶ Ask each child to sign the rules list at the bottom.
>
> ▶ Post the rules in a visible place.
>
> ▶ Develop a list of consequences for breaking the rules.
>
> ▶ Enforce the rules!

③ Blow the cover on bullying.

Don't be afraid to discuss bullying openly. When the issue is out in the open, it is much less likely to occur. And, if it does happen, it won't go unnoticed. Ask your kids general questions about bullying:

Try Saying This:

"What is bullying?"

"How do people feel when they are bullied?"

"How do you think bullies feel?"

"Is there anyone who thinks we have a problem here?"

"What do you think about having a bully-free group?"

If bullying is going on in your group, it isn't necessary to name names. The group as a whole has tremendous power to influence its members. Peer pressure is frequently viewed as a negative means of control. We worry about the peer group's ability to sway its members into actions that are anti-social and destructive. This is not always the case, however. Harnessing the positive influence of the group is an extremely useful skill for the adult leader. Blowing the cover on bullies allows the group to pull together to "out" bullies. The group patrols itself, squashing attempts by bullies to manipulate and control.

Michele, my daughter's soccer coach, exhibited her own version of "blowing the cover on bullying" during a game I witnessed recently. One of the stronger players, Lindsey, was in the habit of putting her fellow team members down every time a mistake was made on the field. "You always mess up," she'd yell. "How could you miss that goal? Are you blind?" At halftime, Michele pulled Lindsey off to the side to say, "You were really mean to your teammates. Everybody on this team makes mistakes. If you do that again, I'll need to pull you out for the rest of the game." Even though Michele did not embarrass Lindsey in front of the team, the girls were aware that she was being called on her bad behavior by their coach. This was a powerful message to the girls to treat each other with respect.

4 Create a "Things Bullies Do" list.

Ask the kids to come up with a list of typical bullying behaviors. Initially, the kids may be tempted to list the stereotypical behaviors they've seen on television or in movies. Stealing lunch money, pushing kids into lockers, and beating kids up are common examples. The children need to know that bullying encompasses a wide spectrum of behaviors. If you are a classroom teacher, you may want to break up your class into small groups and have each group write down as many examples as they can think of. If you are a coach, you may want to have an open discussion with the team.

Things Bullies Do

- **Social alienation** – purposefully and consistently ignoring others to make them feel left out

- **Verbal aggression** – abusing others by name calling and put downs

- **Racism** – attacking people because of race, religion, gender, and/or family background, etc.

- **Ganging up** – enlisting several children to intimidate one child

---

Things Bullies Do (cont'd)

▶ **Gossip** – circulating destructive rumors

▶ **Threatening** – terrorizing someone with the threat of physical or emotional harm

▶ **Sexual harassment** – making threats of a sexual nature where refusal has negative consequences

▶ **Extortion** – getting kids to pay them money, "or else."

 Keep your eyes open.

Jack's camp counselors may not have been aware that there was bullying going on in their bunk. However, it was their responsibility to recognize the potential for bullying in the bunk *before* it started. Sometimes, an early warning sign of bullying is social withdrawal on the part of the victim. Keep a look out for the child who isolates himself. The child who feels bullied may really want to establish friendships within the group, but he'll retreat when he feels this goal is unattainable.

Take a few minutes to check in with your group members individually, especially those who appear withdrawn. It's not difficult to say, "Hey, I notice you have become quieter recently. Sometimes kids do that when they are upset or have been hurt. Is there anything on your mind that you want to talk to me about?"

6 Notice the differences between preference and exclusion.

Not all boys in a bunk are going to like each other. Kids will naturally gravitate toward those they like and want to spend time with. In Jack's case, there were boys in his bunk who clearly did not like him. Preferring to be with other boys is not a crime. But name calling, tripping, and purposeful exclusion are another matter. Jack's counselors were not sensitive to when the behaviors crossed over into abuse. Keep in mind that bullying can quickly escalate when it is not squashed early on.

Reminder

**Nip early signs of bullying
in the bud as soon
as you see them.**

7 Take all accounts of bullying seriously.

If a child reports bullying, you must follow up (even if you secretly feel the accusation is unfounded). The minute you blow off a report of bullying, you nonverbally communicate to the child, "You may as well stop reporting bullying to me because I'm not going to take it seriously."

There will be times when you won't want to listen to an account of bullying – perhaps the timing is bad or there are a lot of other kids around. At those times, try saying the following:

Try Saying This:

"Hey, I hear what you're telling me about bullying. This is not a good time for us to talk about it. I am interested in what you have to say. How about if we talk after the game?"

Reminder

**There is a difference
between reporting on
bullying and tattling.**

A child who complains that another child called him a name, threw water on him, or stepped on his foot is not being bullied. These are isolated incidents. In these situations, which will occur frequently with any group of kids, express your confidence in the group's ability as a whole to resolve minor squabbles independently.

8 Keep your own bullying impulses in check.

Children are very perceptive about an adult's feelings about a child. When you're frustrated with a child who is exhibiting annoying behavior, be extra careful of how you're expressing that in front of the group. Kids love to be given what they perceive as implicit permission to scapegoat. In Jack's case, his counselors may have felt that Jack deserved the treatment he was getting from the other boys. In fact, they may have been subtly colluding with the bullying by not stopping it.

Reminder

**Sometimes inaction
is action!**

9 Cushion the victim.

Make sure that a child who's the target of bullying is surrounded by respectful and empathetic peers. You can do this by asking the at-risk child to partner up with a confident, social group member in a cooperative activity. Bullies are less likely to bother a child when he is surrounded by others.

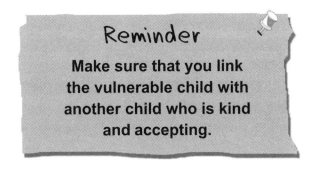

Reminder

Make sure that you link the vulnerable child with another child who is kind and accepting.

How to Help the Victim of Bullying

Kids who are targets of bullying just want to know what to do! They'll look to you for leadership. Unfortunately, many of us have forgotten how we dealt with bullying when we were kids, if we remember being bullied at all! When an upset child comes to us with tales of teasing woe, we so desperately want to fix it that we are compelled to offer them the vast arsenal of our coping techniques: "Just ignore it!" Oh, if it were only that simple. We naively hope that ignoring teasing will solve the problem – the teasing will stop, and we won't have to deal with any more tales of woe. Wrong! Ignoring is rarely a successful method for coping. Children can only ignore teasing for a limited period of time, and when they can't manage it any longer, they blow up. Tears! Upset! Rage! This reaction is *precisely* what the bully is waiting for. Enjoying the control the teaser has over his prey, the bully is fueled for more teasing, leaving the victim feeling helpless to change the situation.

The following pages provide a list of techniques for dealing with bullying that you can suggest to your group of youngsters. Some of these ideas seem so simple you'll wonder how they could possibly be effective. But by and large, all you need are the following variables for the ideas to work:

- ▶ Have a plan.

- ▶ Put the plan into action.

- ▶ Communicate a sense of strength.

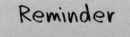

Reminder

Tell your kids to "mix and match" these techniques. If one doesn't work for them, encourage them to try another.

 ## Perfect the "dirty look."

For those kids who are not very verbal or who feel uncomfortable with a verbal comeback, a smirk or a dirty look can be a powerful response.

2 Learn the "short-and-sweet" comeback.

Especially for the younger child, simple, specific verbal responses can be handy. Older kids may have an easier time coming up with words on the spot. Simple words and phrases can be surprisingly effective.

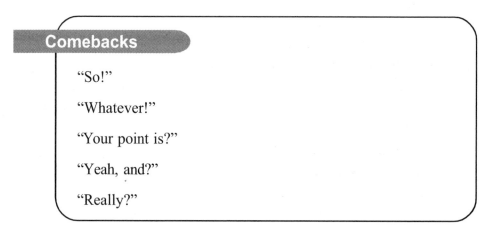

Comebacks

"So!"

"Whatever!"

"Your point is?"

"Yeah, and?"

"Really?"

Comebacks (cont'd)

"Oh well. What can I say? You've said it all."

"You are really enjoying yourself right now. Aren't you?"

"Yeah, right."

"Let me know when you get to the funny part."

Keep in mind that some children are just not "comeback" kids. If these kids get into a comeback war with a bully, they will lose the battle (and the war!). For these kids, it is *crucial* that after they've delivered their comeback phrase, they should immediately *walk away*. This is not the child who should stick around waiting for a reaction from the bully.

I'll never forget a little boy I worked with in a group several years ago. Lee was getting teased mercilessly in school. A small, timid boy, Lee had no idea how to respond when the other kids put him down – he would just respond to an attack with an attack of his own. The problem is that this method served only to anger the bullies more and increase their aggressive behavior. Lee learned in his social skills training group that his best response to this situation was a simple retort. A word or two said in a confident manner, followed by a quick exit, seemed to do the trick.

3 Confront whispering directly.

Part of the power of whispering is that it is underhanded and indirect. By challenging it directly with, "Do you have something you want to say to me?" the child is not allowing the whispering to go on without comment. Kids who gossip and whisper do so partly because they believe they can get away with it. Confronting the behavior directly and without emotion, although challenging, often puts a stop to the whispering.

4 Articulate the obvious.

When a child in your group is being provoked, ask him to respond simply by pointing out, without judgment, what the other child is doing that is bothering him. Rather than saying, "Stop it! You're annoying me," (usually said in a whiny voice) he could say, "You are kicking my chair." By stating the obvious, calmly, the provocative child has the chance to save face and stop kicking.

⑤ Ask a distracting question.

This technique can only be used on occasion. However, when used sparingly, it can be very disarming. When a group is ganging up on a child, he turns directly to them and innocently asks, "Do you have the time?" Then, he walks away! The group is so surprised by the question that they stop teasing, giving the victim a chance to make his exit.

⑥ Acknowledge mistakes and move on.

This is an especially useful technique to use when the child is criticized for making a mistake during a game or while answering a question in school. First, remind the child that everyone makes mistakes and that mistakes help us learn. Then, persuade the child to practice responding to teasing by saying, "You're right. I blew it. I'll get it right next time." Even if the child doesn't say this out loud, saying it in his head can help him move on from the event.

⑦ Laugh it off.

Laugh at yourself often. Kids love to see that adults can laugh at themselves too. As long as both parties involved find the teasing funny, it's okay to poke fun. Benign teasing and laughing about it can become part of the culture of the group.

⑧ Turn the table on the teaser.

A child can make another child feel silly for teasing as long as he doesn't resort to counter-attacks. The goal is to take away the power from the teaser by viewing his teasing as immature or inane. Here are some good retorts to use:.

Retorts

"That's an old one."

"You think I haven't heard that one before?"

"Is that all you could come up with?"

"Whoa. Now, you're just scaring me." (said sarcastically)

"Tell me something I haven't heard before."

How to Handle the Bully

Sometimes no matter how hard you try to set the stage to prevent bullying, it still occurs. Whether they happen in the classroom, on the field, in your bunk, or at your meetings, these situations are tricky to manage appropriately. Should you meet with the kids as a group? Do you talk to the victim alone? Do you call the parents? The following plan will help you figure out the best approach to cope with bullying.

① Get information from other adult observers.

Use your adult resources to validate the information you have received. If you are a teacher, you might check in with the cafeteria workers, the P.E. teachers, or other professionals that see the kids during unstructured times. If you are a camp counselor, check in with your co-counselors or activities leaders. If the other adults haven't noticed anything unusual, ask them to pay special attention and report what they see. You'll want to know not only what is happening, but exactly who is involved. Is there a ringleader? Who are the bystanders?

② Talk to the bullied child in private.

Inquire gently into the feelings of the victim. Without judgment and using a neutral tone, see if you can find out who is involved in the situation.

③ Meet individually with each child involved.

Arrange a private meeting with each participant. Make sure the sessions are back-to-back. You'll want to minimize the potential for peer pressure if the kids gather to discuss the situation. In each meeting, you can act as a neutral facilitator by inviting each child to consider his role in the bullying. Then ask each child to develop a plan for improving the situation. Maintaining the focus on each individual's role is an effective way to ensure that each child takes responsibility for his actions.

④ Meet as a group.

In this meeting, the group focuses on solving the problem. Each participant talks about the ways that he believes he can change his behavior to help improve the situation. Then, encourage the kids to put their heads together to come up with a group plan. All suggestions should be met with approval and support.

⑤ Set a time to follow up.

Set a date for a follow-up talk in the next week. This meeting can be brief – the goal is to make sure the group is accountable to their previous agreement. If the bullying has indeed stopped, give *all* the kids lots of kudos!

⑥ Do periodic check-ins.

Every couple of weeks, check in with the entire group to make sure that the agreed upon goals continue to be met.

Meeting with the Victim (Jack)

You: "Hey, Jack, I understand you've been having a hard time with some of the kids in your bunk. Do you want to tell me about the situation?"

Jack: "It's Christopher and Anthony. They are really nasty to me. I tell them to stop, but they just keep right on teasing me."

You: "You sound pretty upset. Is there anything you can think of that might help the situation?"

Jack: "I've tried everything. I've tried ignoring them. I've tried yelling at them. I've even tried pushing them, but it just keeps happening. The only time they leave me alone is when I'm with Justin."

You: "So, when you hang out with one of your friends, they leave you alone."

Jack: "Yeah, Justin is cool. He's got my back."

You: "So, he is pretty protective of you?"

Jack: "Yeah!"

You: "I guess you've got to make sure you've got your 'protector' nearby more often. Hey, Jack, do you think there is anything you are doing that may be contributing to Christopher and Anthony's bad feelings about you?"

Jack: "Well, when they are mean to me, it just makes me want to keep bugging them."

You: "If you stop bugging them, do you think it would help you or hurt you?"

Jack: "Well, I guess it would help."

You: "Why don't you give it a shot? And, we'll check back on this a week from now."

Meeting with the Bystander (Tyler)

You: "Hey, Tyler, I understand that there is some teasing going on in the bunk. Do you know anything about it?"

Tyler: "Yeah, I've noticed that Jack really annoys Christopher and Anthony! They are really rough on him though. Jack doesn't bother me. When he's annoying, I just let it go. It only bugs me when we're all trying to get to sleep."

You: "I know you don't join in with Christopher and Anthony when they give Jack a hard time. I'm glad to see that. But, can you think of something you could do to help the situation in the future?"

Tyler: "Yeah, I guess I could tell Christopher and Anthony. They usually listen to me."

You: "Good idea, Tyler!"

Meeting with the Bully (Christopher)

You: "Hey, Christopher, I am hearing that there is some pretty nasty stuff happening in this bunk. What do you know about it?"

Christopher: "It's Jack. He is so annoying! He totally keeps us awake when we are trying to sleep. He gets in my face and won't stop. He's such an idiot!"

Try Saying This (cont'd):

You: "I can tell you are pretty frustrated with Jack. But, you know, Christopher, we don't call people 'idiots' in our bunk. And, the word around the bunk is that you and Anthony are pretty mean to Jack. Jack has been pretty upset about it."

Christopher: "Well, then, he should stop being so annoying. If he stopped, we wouldn't have to be so mean."

You: "Nobody 'makes you' act mean, Christopher. You are responsible for your own actions. This situation is really upsetting Jack. What can you do to improve the situation? And, Christopher, I am going to ask this same question of Anthony and Jack so that they can also tell me what each of them could do differently to improve this situation."

Christopher: "Okay. I won't be mean anymore."

You: "Excellent. So, you'll treat Jack with respect from here on out. Let's meet again in a week or so to see how you're doing on this."

⑦ Meet the parents.

If the warning signs of bullying are there, and your impressions are corroborated by others, it's time to inform the parents. Telling parents that their child exhibits bullying behavior is awkward and needs to be handled delicately. No parent wants to hear that their child is a bully. You must convey your concern about their child's behavior without using labels or put-downs. Whenever possible, it's best to talk to parents about their child in person, rather than by phone or e-mail. Always begin the conversation by noting their child's positive qualities. You can expect that the parents, at first, will be defensive. Stick to reporting the bullying behaviors you and other adults have observed. Look to the parents for help in resolving the problem.

Try Saying This:

You: "Mr. Smith, I wanted to meet with you today about Colin. I really like Colin. He's one of my best players. He puts his all into the sport, and I can always count on him to bring the team back from the brink. However, there is a situation on the team that does concern me."

Mr. Smith: "Really? What's happening?"

You: "Recently, I've seen some evidence that Colin may be bullying one of the kids on the team."

Mr. Smith: "Bullying? Colin? C'mon. You can't be serious."

You: "Yes, I am serious. There is one kid in particular that he seems to have problems with. The other day, he tripped him when he thought I wasn't looking. And, in the locker room last week, I walked in as Colin was harassing this same kid about a missed play. These kinds of things have happened five or six times, and the other child is threatening to quit the team. I tried talking to Colin about it, but he blew me off. Do you think you can help me on this one? This kind of situation is a downer for the team."

Mr. Smith: "Well, I'll talk to him about it."

You: "Thanks, Mr. Smith. I really appreciate your help on this. I'll give you a call next week to check in on Colin's reaction and see what the two of you figured out."

Reminder

Create a positive, supportive atmosphere where bullying won't be tolerated.

Cooperation
Working as a Team

There is a subtle difference between cooperation and compliance. When kids are compliant, they are submitting to adult will, which often leads to power struggles. Cooperation, on the other hand, means that kids are able to work in tandem to achieve a common goal that is mutually satisfying for all. Distinguishing between the two is critical to achieving cooperation within a kids' group. To develop a cooperative atmosphere in a group, kids must buy in to the essential need for rules, plans, and adult requests. They understand that without guidelines, the group as a whole fails.

There are steps you can take to help your group cooperate more openly, and there are certain behaviors to steer clear of if you want to avoid power struggles and loss of control in the group.

This is Julie's last year as a school bus driver. She's burned out. Every day after work she complains to her husband about the kids. "This is the WORST bunch I've ever had. They don't listen to anything I say. They are out of control, and I'm scared I'm going to get in an accident one of these days." Julie believes the kids are spoiled and undisciplined. She's astonished that they don't respect her authority as an adult, and she's convinced that since she first started driving a bus 10 years ago, the kids' behavior has gotten worse with each passing year.

Julie tries to manage the kids' behavior by:

▶ *Yelling at them: "Sit down now!"*

▶ *Threatening them: "If you don't stop it, I'm going to report you!"*

▶ *Ignoring their behavior completely*

▶ *Pleading with them: "C'mon guys…"*

▶ *Lecturing them: "I have never seen such a bad group. Do you know what would have happened to me if I had behaved like this growing up?"*

None of Julie's methods seems to be working. She's decided to throw in the towel rather than go on coping with the stress of these badly behaved kids.

I know that most of you are not bus drivers. But, like Julie, as a leader of a group of children, you must create an atmosphere in your group where cooperation takes place. The steps outlined below can be applied in any group of kids, whether you are a Boy Scout leader, a camp counselor, or a teacher. For that matter, managing a group of kids is not much different from leading a team of adults in a work setting. Nobody wants to work under a dictator! Good managers lead their team, and the team wants to follow. Here are some steps you can take to encourage cooperation:

① Expect cooperation.

It may sound corny, but if you want kids to cooperate with you, you have to believe they *will* cooperate with you. Your belief in the kids' ability to work together cooperatively is imperative. The kids will take their cues from you.

② Praise kids for their cooperative efforts.

Your words and your tone of voice are very important. Always be specific with praise, and make sure that you praise the group immediately after you witness cooperative behavior. When you reward the entire group for positive interactions, everyone is more motivated to work together peaceably. For instance, perhaps Julie could have focused on her group's movement in the right direction, rather than on their bad behavior.

Try Saying This:

"I notice that almost everyone is in their seats, as I asked. If each of you can be in your seat by the time I beep the horn, each of you will get a surprise before you get off the bus today!"

"You all quieted down the first time I asked. I really appreciate that, guys!"

"Yesterday, you two had a big argument, and today, you are both making an effort to get along. It's hard work sometimes to maintain friendship!"

 ## Use the S.O.A.R. method in your group.

We use this method in our groups to encourage cooperation and highlight positive social interactions. The S.O.A.R. approach includes the following steps:

S –   Stop Action

O –   Observe Aloud

A –   Ask for Feedback

R –   Reinforce Cooperative Interaction

Freeze action during a group activity to observe out loud cooperative efforts. Watch how this technique empowers the group to cooperate!

S (Stop Action):   "Hey guys, let's freeze for a second here."

O (Observe Aloud):   "Is anyone noticing how great this group is all working together right now to get this goal accomplished?"

A (Ask for Feedback):   "How great does it feel to work so well together as a team? If you like it, yell 'Yes'!"

R (Reinforce Cooperative Action): "What great teamwork!"

4 Help your kids tune in to their behavior.

A basic component of good cooperation is the ability to observe oneself and change behavior to fit the demands of a particular situation. Kids rebel against rules when they don't understand them or when they are imposed unpredictably.

Try Saying This:

"How are we doing as a group? Thumbs up if you think we are following the group rules!"

"Let's check in with how we are doing today. How do you think the group is doing on meeting group goals?"

"I notice something happening in the group right now. Can you guess what it is that I see?"

5 Let kids know your expectations of them in advance.

If kids are made aware of behavioral guidelines and expectations in advance of situations, they feel more a part of the decision-making process. This encourages them to take responsibility for their own actions. As an adult, you are more able to anticipate potential problems in the group. By using this technique, you are helping the kids anticipate and manage potential problems with you.

Try Saying This:

"Okay, guys. We're getting off the bus in three minutes. What are the three rules we must follow when getting off the bus?"

"Before we begin, I need to remind you that you must stay in your seat and keep your hands and feet to yourself."

"Last time we were all together, behavior got really rowdy by the end of the group. What behavior will we see this week at the end of the group?"

---

6 Describe the problem.

Like Julie did, it's tempting for us to try to enlist cooperation from kids by first telling them what to do. And then, when they don't respond right away, we resort to threatening, yelling, sarcasm, belittling, and lecturing. Tempting? Yes. Successful? Not so much!

Given the fact that kids are going to have to be told more than once to do what's expected of them, it's important to find ways to communicate our wishes without nagging or doing damage to their self-esteem. Describing the problem unemotionally is one way. The following are suggestions for Julie's situation:

Try Saying This:	Rather Than This:
"I see people standing in the aisles."	"How many times do I have to tell you guys to sit down?"
"I can't concentrate on driving when there is so much yelling."	"Shut Up!!"
"I see kids on each others' laps."	"Jill! Get off Suzie's lap! Now!!"

Keep your descriptions short and sweet. If you can give a direction with one word, do it! For example:

"Gloves!"

"School books!"

"Scripts!"

7 Use "I" messages.

When you say "I feel…" rather than "You did…" or "You are a …," you are more likely to get cooperation and less likely to make someone defensive and resistant. Read the following statements. Which ones sound better to you?

Try Saying This:	Rather Than This:
"I feel disregarded when you ignore what I'm saying."	"You never listen!"
"I feel taken advantage of when you leave your snack wrappers everywhere for others to pick up."	"You guys are a bunch of slobs!"
"I'm really upset that you threw that ball in here, someone could have gotten hurt."	"You could have killed someone!"

> ## Reminder
>
> **"I feel you are a big jerk"
> is not an appropriate use of
> the "I feel" statement. You
> must follow "I feel..." with
> an actual feeling.**

Give choices.

Give your kids choices without resorting to negotiating with them or break-
ing the rules you've established. Kids of all ages enjoy choices. Begin with
explanations about limits and requests, and point out how a rule benefits the
whole group. After the explanation, provide the choices. This gives the group
a feeling of autonomy and the desire to cooperate.

Try Saying This:

"We have to clean up so that the next time we can find our
stuff. Do you want to sweep or do you want to dust?"

"We are having the cast party at my house. Do you want to
have pizza or hamburgers and hot dogs for dinner?"

"It's time for you to go to bed. Do you want to have time in
bed to read for fifteen minutes or do you want lights out
immediately?"

"Campers, as I see it, you have two choices about morning
wake-up call. I can wake you up quietly at 7:20 a.m. or the
head counselor can blow his whistle at 7:30 a.m. Do you see
any other ways of doing it?"

9 Hold a group meeting.

Group meetings are a wonderful way to help kids develop cooperation skills. These meetings can be used to resolve conflicts, organize group activities, communicate openly about group issues, and establish camaraderie.

> **Establish a regular meeting day and time.** It's important to establish a regular meeting day and time for the group, whether it's once a week, bimonthly, or once a month.

> **Go over structure and ground rules**. It doesn't really matter what the meeting structure is, as long as it's consistent. For instance, some groups have informal meetings where members share issues and concerns in an open forum. Other groups are more structured and organized.

> **Maintain a positive, light tone.** You might be surprised that after a couple of these meetings, the kids actually look forward to getting together to talk and make decisions

> **Do you want to have a note taker?** It might be helpful to have someone from the group take notes so they can be shared at the next gathering. Somehow, when group resolutions are written down, group members take them more seriously. Group notes are also a good way to track issues and maintain follow-through.

> **Do you need to be the meeting facilitator?** As group leader, you do not need to be the meeting facilitator. You may decide that you'd like to rotate this responsibility among the group members.

> **Begin each meeting with a review**. Make sure that previous resolutions are enacted and enforced. If they're not, solutions need to be reviewed again to figure out what's getting in the way of follow-through.

> **Create a list of agenda items.** Ask group members to write down agenda items in advance of a meeting. This gives the kids a chance to mull over the issues. In addition, this gives you the chance to veto any agenda items that may not be appropriate to discuss in the meeting.

▶ **Each member is encouraged to weigh in**. Feeling heard goes a long way in helping the group come to a consensus. Decisions are usually made by consensus. If you get stuck on a particular issue, it can be shelved until the following

week. Sometimes the group needs to sit on something for a few days before they can reach an agreement.

I have found that a debriefing session following any type of group meeting is extremely useful in creating a cooperative environment. We take a few minutes to review the skills we've worked on, highlight positive interactions, and reaffirm the group's goals. I encourage you to carve out a little time at the end of your meetings to do the same.

Reminder

Keep the meetings short and sweet!

Learning how to encourage cooperation instead of demanding compliance takes effort, thoughtfulness, and lots of practice. Once your kids develop trust in you, they are much more likely to cooperate and work together for the benefit of the group as a whole.

Discipline
Establishing Boundaries

Nate looks forward to directing his stepson Matt's school play each year. He sees it as an ongoing opportunity to bond with Matt. Nate has a background in the theatre and enjoys helping the kids create something special on stage. Most of the time, he's able to keep the group engaged in the process of rehearsing and performing. But every year as the big night approaches, the kids become increasingly revved up and unable to rein in their excitement, despite Nate's gentle reminders and urgings: "Okay, everybody, settle down!" "Is everybody listening?" "I need you to listen to me now!" Nate wants to regain control of the group without quelling the kids' enthusiasm, but he's unsure of his role as a disciplinarian. He wants the kids to like him and fears that disciplining them will make him into the "bad guy." However, if he avoids setting limits altogether, the show will surely fall apart completely as the group slides closer to chaos.

Children need limits. They may not *want* them, but they most certainly *need* them. When boundaries are unclear, kids become uncomfortable and push the edges of the envelope, seeking limits. They will continue to push until we let them know clearly when they've hit that edge. Nate's discomfort with setting clear limits and using discipline is a typical problem for adult leaders. It's important to have a few solid, simple techniques ready for those times when you will inevitably need to discipline. Following are some common sense ways to approach discipline with your group:

1 Reverse the negative to positive ratio.

It's much easier to fall into the habit of criticizing rather than praising. When your group is like Nate's – boisterous and full of energy – it can be tricky locating any constructive behavior to reinforce. Nate must work hard to find the behavior he wants to reinforce. But when he does, the praise reverberates throughout the group. He may be surprised to see the kids alter their negative behavior when they see others in the group being praised for pro-social behavior. Nate will want to change from doling out disciplinary statements to some kids, to offering praise statements to others. Watch how quickly the kids' negative behavior changes when they see you praising others in your group. Children naturally want to please and earn praise from adults they respect.

Try Saying This:	Rather Than This:
"I see that John, Gabe, and Sam are all sitting quietly while I speak."	"Alex, sit down! Now!"
"Sarah, Jesse, and Doug, thanks for listening while I give notes. It makes it easier for me."	"Harry, stop talking!"
"We get so much more work done when everyone is focused on the goal. Thanks."	"Cut out the nonsense!"

Your automatic reaction may be to criticize a child who is acting badly. Resist this impulse. Instead, look for another child in your group who is demonstrating the conduct you'd like to see. Praise this child immediately, and watch as the poorly behaving child follows suit. When this happens, make sure you instantly praise the child who changed his behavior from negative to positive!

Reminder

Do not proceed with your group activity until all group members have followed your command.

② **Make your disciplinary statements short and sweet, without harshness.**

Sometimes discipline is necessary. As positive as you are with the kids, from time to time, group members will need adults to actively correct bad behavior. When that happens, take the minimal approach. Keep it clear. Keep it simple. Keep it cool. The kids need to know that you are in charge and in control of the situation. The tone of your voice sends an important message. Take a few deep breaths if it helps you. Just be certain you know how you are feeling before you deliver any criticism or correction. Rather than using the words "don't" or "stop," try the following:

Try Saying This:

"Hey, guys, hands and feet to yourself."

"I'm waiting for quiet so that we can proceed."

"I'd like to see all eyes on me."

"I can't hear when there is so much yelling in here."

Disciplinary Don'ts

- Don't use threats.

- Don't use put-downs or insults.

- Don't yell or curse.

- Don't interrupt.

- Don't be sarcastic.

- Don't lecture.

- Don't arouse guilt.

As leaders, we are all vulnerable to engaging in "Disciplinary Don'ts." My personal Achilles' heel is sarcasm, especially in my work with teenagers. A teenager may be experimenting with sarcasm to express evolving wit, but I know that sarcasm is also an indirect form of communication that frequently hides feelings of hostility, anger, and frustration. As tempted as I am to join adolescents in their sarcastic relay, I must resist and instead express myself directly. For instance, instead of saying to one of my tardy group members, "Congratulations, Shawn, you are only ten minutes late for our meeting today," I would say, "Shawn, our meetings begin promptly at six. Please arrive on time next week."

③ Use effective commands.

Make sure when you give a child a directive that you mean it. Say the command clearly and firmly. Kids know a phony when they see one. If you tell a child to do something, and you have no intention of making sure that the direction is followed, the direction will *not* be followed!!

To become more effective when disciplining, try the following steps:

▶ Give the command.

▶ Wait silently for compliance (at least 30 seconds).

▶ Impose an immediate consequence if the command is not followed.

▶ For instance, "Stop bouncing that ball." (Wait 30 seconds) If the bouncing continues, "Next time you bounce the ball, I will have to take it from you." (Wait 30 seconds) If the bouncing still continues, "I have to take the ball because you have shown me you can't stop bouncing it."

Reminder

Make sure you have the child's attention before you give the command. If a child is looking at you straight in the eye, you have his attention.

④ Tell the kids what you want them to do, not just what you don't want them to do.

Establish the behavioral expectations for your group at the get-go. The clearer you can be up front with your vision of their behavior, the easier it is for the group to make appropriate choices. Then, when they do struggle (which they will), you'll have a structure and guidelines to fall back on. It is not enough to just say "Stop!" or "Don't." Group members may also need explicit instructions. Help the kids replace bad behavior with alternative positive choices.

"I know you can make the right choice next time. I wonder if next time you can try…"

"Tell me about the problem you're having using a calm voice. I know you can do it."

"I need to take this phone call. Please continue to practice using the same strategies we've been using the last half hour."

"We treat each other with respect in this group. I expect the same of you."

Reminder

When emotions run high, it is even harder to maintain self-control.

 ## 5 Put responsibilities before rewards.

Work first. Play later. My parents lived by this credo and enforced it with my brother, sister, and me. "You must finish your homework *before* you go out and play." "You must clean your room *before* you leave for basketball practice." "You must earn some money *before* you can spend it." Now I can see how invaluable it is to establish a strong work ethic in our kids. While I was growing up, I just wanted to skip to the playing part. I wanted to skip the responsibilities and get straight to the reward.

The "You must…..before you" method of establishing self-discipline is a powerful one. Kids learn that rewards come as a direct result of fulfilling responsibility. When kids fall down on the job, there is no reward. Simple as that!

You must ...	Before you ...
set up your campsite...	go down to the water and fish.
run the track eight times...	play in practice today.
pass in your completed homework...	go out to play at recess.
clean the bunk...	have "free period."

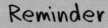

Reminder

When a child doesn't earn the privilege or reward for fulfilling a responsibility, empathize with his feelings of disappointment but, whatever you do, follow through on your initial directive.

 6 ## Set logical consequences.

In addition to setting a standard for group behavior in advance, you must also define the consequences if rules are broken and limits are tested. Logical consequences should be directly related to the misbehavior exhibited. They are the real-life results of bad behavior. Nate might tell his kids that those who misbehave and use up the director's valuable time will have to stay after rehearsal to help the director clean the stage. Kids need to know that their choices have direct results which affect them.

Try these consequences!

Since you ...	Then you ...
fooled around throughout the last practice…	can't play until the last quarter of the game.
were late for rehearsal…	have to stay late to clean up the props.
are wasting my time by fooling around...	owe me time at the end of practice.
kept your bunkmates awake last night…	have to go to bed early this evening.

Reminder

As with expectations, consequences will differ depending upon the age of the group members.

 7 Divide and conquer.

Frequently, it is not *all* of the group members who are misbehaving. It may be a handful of kids who are stirring each other up. In this case, it may be helpful to separate the offenders. Link them up with peers who are both socially appropriate and good leaders in the group. In the case of the school play, Nate could break his rehearsal up into several small groups of kids to practice their lines, making sure to keep the over-excited cast members apart from each other for a time.

My nine-year-old nephew, Daniel, told me about how his basketball coach used this technique. The coach saw that some of his team members concentrated during practice, while others used the time to goof off. According to Daniel, the coach separated the goof-offs from each other and had them practice with more serious members of the team. Then, the coach rewarded the focused players by allowing them to play earlier and stay longer in the game. As each team member's negative behavior improved, he was also allowed the privilege of getting into the game sooner and playing longer. Daniel thought this was a successful way to handle a difficult situation.

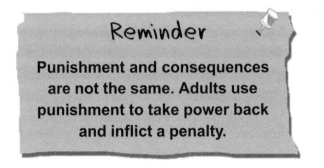

Reminder

Punishment and consequences are not the same. Adults use punishment to take power back and inflict a penalty.

⑧ Hold a time-out or a cooling off period.

Time-out may be the most overused parenting strategy out there. It's also commonly misused. Adults often automatically resort to using time-out when

they really don't know what else to do. This confuses kids who then view a time-out as a punishment for misbehaving, rather than a valuable tool for them to regain the ability to interact with others appropriately, follow directions or stick to the rules.

It is important that you stay very calm when you deliver a time-out. Make certain that you explain to the child why the time-out is necessary by connecting it to the problem behavior.

"Because of the way you acted on the field just now, you need to sit on the bench until you can calm down."

"One of our class rules is to keep hands and feet to ourselves. Because you couldn't do that, you've lost the privilege of being with your friends at recess until you can show me you've pulled yourself together."

"Since you've broken the bunk rule of 'no food fights,' you'll have to sit by yourself at lunchtime for the rest of the week."

9 Maintain consistency and follow-through.

What's that expression? "Mean what you say, and say what you mean." There really is no way for a child to understand this concept unless you are unwavering in enforcing rules and consequences. Holding kids accountable for their actions is really no different from what we do with our work colleagues every day. It's easy to establish office rules and expectations, but it's harder to make sure they are being followed. If no one in authority 1) makes sure the policies and procedures are being followed, and 2) holds workers accountable if they are not, organizations would suffer and ultimately collapse. It's the same with kids. Establish the guiding principles up front, but then make sure they are being followed and that the consequences for transgressions are reliable and consistent.

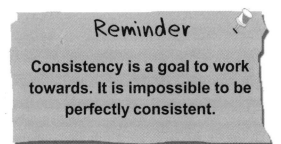

Reminder

Consistency is a goal to work towards. It is impossible to be perfectly consistent.

Maintaining discipline in your group may be challenging, but the strategies outlined above can help you manage your group more easily and effectively. Give them a try!

Empathy
Seeking Another's Perspective

"You stink!" Carlos shouted. "I'm always stuck on his team," Joseph grumbled. Patrick doesn't know what to say when the boys are mean to him like this. He wants to play with the rest of the class, but he hates that every time he kicks the ball, someone catches it. He sulks off the field, red-faced and humiliated after messing up. Usually, there are no teachers present at the recess game. But today, Mr. Eck, the P.E. teacher, just happens to be nearby on the blacktop. "Hey, guys. Team huddle!" he calls. The boys reluctantly gather around Mr. Eck. "Who saw what just happened?" he asks. Hector says, "I did. Carlos and Joseph pretty much told Patrick he stinks." "Okay, guys. Anybody have any guesses as to how Patrick is feeling right now?" asks Mr. Eck. Several boys answer, "Mad!" "Sad!" "Embarrassed!" "I think you guys are absolutely right. That's how I'd feel if someone told me I stink. Do we want to make each other feel bad?" asks Mr. Eck. The whole group says, "No!" "Let's get back to the game, guys. And remember that we always treat our teammates with respect. No matter what. Okay?"

One of your primary goals as a leader is to help your kids understand and respect the needs and feelings of others in the group. The ability to empathize, however, is a highly complex skill. Empathy is defined as the capacity to feel and think what another feels and thinks by observing verbal and non-verbal cues. The following list describes the behaviors of someone who can empathize:

A Person with Empathy:

- ▶ Concentrates on what the other person is saying.

- ▶ Notices the behavior of the other person and tries to understand what is being communicated by that behavior.

- ▶ Imagines the feelings of the other person.

- ▶ Responds appropriately.

Yikes! This may seem like a pretty complicated process. It's no wonder that so many children (and adults) struggle with it. In Patrick's case, Carlos and Joseph are not sensitive to the potential impact their words have on Patrick. In order for them to do that, they need to "stand in Patrick's shoes." This is called perspective-taking. Mr. Eck helps the boys look at the situation through Patrick's eyes to try to imagine how Patrick might be feeling. This helps the boys empathize with Patrick.

Helping Children Develop Empathy

The following is a series of steps for you to help your group members develop empathy. This is one area where highlighting specific examples and modeling appropriate behavior are extremely effective.

1 **Pay attention to the way your group members interact.**

Begin by paying attention to group dynamics. Ask yourself questions like, "Who is the group's leader?" "Is there anyone in the group being ignored?" "How are the kids interacting with the new group members?" It's very important that you build an atmosphere of trust and inclusion. Watch out for kids who appear to be ostracized, especially in groups of girls.

② Prompt the kids to think about the feelings and reactions of others.

Ask your group to think about the needs of others. Make sure you react calmly to what they say in response, and listen completely to their responses before you offer your opinion. The kids need to feel that their perspectives are valued, even if you don't see things exactly the same way.

Try Saying This:

"How do you think Jamal felt when Marcus pushed him?"

"Why do you think Amanda didn't want Jennifer to play with her?"

"Who in the group is making a special effort to get to know our new member?"

③ Help the kids develop a larger, more detailed vocabulary of feelings.

I can't overestimate the value for children of understanding their own feelings and being able to express them in a clear, calm fashion. Kids with healthy social behaviors tend to have a solid understanding of their own feelings, which helps them tune in to others' feelings.

It isn't necessary for you to sit down and formally define a range of feelings to your kids. Simply by demonstrating and verbalizing a variety of feelings yourself, you are modeling the importance of understanding your own and other people's emotions. You could express yourself like this:

"I find it frustrating when I talk and you don't listen."

"It really pushes my buttons and makes me angry when I see you treating each other with disrespect."

"I am truly grateful to be working with such a terrific group of kids."

"I am as disappointed as you are that our game is rained out."

④ Help the kids tune in to body language and facial expressions.

Learning this skill can be a lot of fun. Help your kids understand the motivations and feelings of others by observing out loud what others' faces and bodies are saying. Highlight for them the clues people give us to show what they are feeling. For example, notice how red faces and loud voices show anger, or how wide-open eyes and mouths show surprise. You might want to talk with your kids about what the facial expressions would look like for each of the feelings listed at the end of this chapter.

Try Saying This:

"Molly is trying to show us something with her body right now. What is it that you think she is saying to us?"

"I've just separated Jamal and Marcus. Why do you think I did that? What were they feeling just then?"

"I can see by your faces that you are unhappy with that decision."

Try "freezing action" in your group. Ask your kids to remain frozen while they look around the group and observe aloud what they see. Facial expressions and body poses reveal a lot about how someone is feeling.

⑤ Encourage a sense of humor.

It's common knowledge that laughing is a healing emotion. Think about how good you feel after a long, hearty laugh. It's the same for kids. But it's often hard to maintain a sense of humor. Many things can cause stress in a child's life, such as academic and peer pressures. You can help your kids see the funny side of life. Share jokes with them. Tell funny stories. And most importantly, teach your kids to laugh at themselves by laughing at your own foibles. The next time you make a mistake, point it out and laugh out loud at yourself. Help your group to see that mistakes are a part of life – it's okay to make them, learn from them, and move on.

There are some kids who take the actions of others too seriously – these are the kids who have the most trouble with teasing and bullies. Help these kids notice when actions are benign rather than malevolent. Even though this won't always be the case, it doesn't hurt to assume there was no evil intent before jumping to conclusions. Help the kids practice laughing off situations, and I guarantee you'll see it result in better relationships for them.

6 Teach your kids to respond empathetically to others.

Even if a child doesn't clearly understand the nuances expressed by others, it's still important that he respond *as if* he understands. For instance, if Sam tells Aaron that he had a fight with his brother, and Aaron doesn't really understand what they were fighting about, it's still important for Aaron to act as if he understands by appearing to be listening, nodding his head, and having a caring facial expression. It often happens that acting as if you understand can actually lead to understanding. If you act as if you are confident, for instance, in time you may actually feel confident. If you act as if you are sympathetic to someone else's problem, in time you may actually feel sympathetic.

In this vein, teach your kids to say short words that express empathy.

Short Words that Express Empathy

"Oh" (said in a disappointed tone)

"Uh Oh"

"Wow!"

"Oh no!"

Help them to maintain a facial expression and body stance that appears caring. Work with the group to come up with a list of words and expressions that demonstrate empathetic listening. Gradually begin teaching your group to ask follow-up questions that help open up others instead of close them down. If you don't feel comfortable teaching the kids these skills, the next best option is to demonstrate empathy yourself.

Statements that Shut Down Communication

"So?"

"That's no big deal. That happens to me all the time."

"Why are you so upset about that?"

Questions that Open Up Others

"What's bothering you?"

"Do you want to talk about it?"

"How can I help you?"

"Can you tell me what happened?"

When you see a child acting as if he's empathizing, reward him with specific praise.

"I like when I see you take care of each other like that."

"I bet Maggie feels heard when you listen to her so carefully."

"I really feel like you are listening to me when you look at me when I'm talking to you."

If you are really feeling creative, there are even games and exercises you can play with your group that encourage empathy and perspective-taking. Give them a try!

Empathy Games and Exercises

Picture Viewing

Look at picture books or at ads in a magazine. Write captions to go with the expressions. Make comments about each face.

Story Reading

Read a story to the group. Stop often and discuss how the characters in a story might be feeling.

TV/Movie Watching

Watch a TV show or a movie together with the kids. Pause and discuss what the characters might be feeling and how they're communicating their feelings.

The "Guess the Feeling" Game

Have your kids stand in front of the group and express feelings. Have the other group members guess the feeling and comment on whether the feelings were clearly expressed. The goal of this game is to guess the feelings behind the body language.

The Hat Trick Game

Put pieces of paper with different feelings written on them inside one hat. (Hat #1 will contain papers saying "happy," "sad," "scared," "frustrated," "excited," "angry," and so on.) Put pieces of paper with tasks written on them inside another hat. (Hat #2's papers will read "say hello to friend," "take off your coat," "ask a friend over to hang out," and so on.) Have one of the kids choose one "feeling" and one "task" from each hat. The object of the game is to perform the tasks while conveying the feeling. Others must guess what the feelings are. The goal of the game is for kids to increase their awareness of others' feelings and for the performer to express feelings more clearly. You can increase the level of difficulty by making the feelings more challenging.

The People Watching Game

Sit in a good people watching spot with your group members. Observe people going by, and say out loud together what you think people's facial expressions and body language are communicating. Try to make up stories about people based on their appearance. Ask questions like, "Where do you think that person is going?" Notice the cues that let us understand how others feel. Then wonder aloud about their motivations. "Why do you think that child is crying?" Highlight for your group the clues people give us to tell us what they're feeling. "Notice that her face is red, her voice is loud, and her jaw is clenched. That woman must be angry!"

The Videotape Exercise

Tape your group without them knowing about it. Sometimes children have no idea how they appear to others. Whenever we videotape the kids in our social skills training groups, most of them are amazed at what they see on the tape. "I can't believe I did that!" This technique allows kids to see themselves through others' eyes and helps them alter their future actions.

The Tape Recording Game

Tape yourself with a tape recorder saying the same word repeatedly, but use a different tone of voice each time you say it. Play it back for your kids and see if they can differentiate what the feeling is behind each word. For instance, if you choose the word *stay*, first say it in an angry way, then in a firm but unemotional way, then as if you are asking a question, then as if you are frustrated, and so on. This exercise is harder than it seems. Give it a try!

The "Feeling of the Day" Exercise

To help your kids learn more about feelings, teach a "Feeling of the Day." Begin with simple ones, like *mad, sad, glad*, and move on to more challenging ones like *frustrated, disappointed*, and *confused*. (See the box below for a list of feelings to review.) I find it helpful to post the Feeling of the Day in an obvious place, such as on a bulletin board. Use the word in sentences regularly throughout the day, and point it out to the kids if someone exhibits that feeling.

Feelings List					
mad	sad	glad	happy	disappointed	angry
upset	confused	frustrated	satisfied	interested	loving
silly	stressed	bored	pleased	thoughtful	shocked
dreamy	guilty	scared	sick	affectionate	excited
shy	surprised	irritable	lonely	embarrassed	anxious
grouchy	brave	jealous	tired	proud	worried

Empathy skills can be taught. You will see that with empathy and an increased awareness of the feelings of others, your kids will become closer to each other. Children need to know that they are understood. Take an active role in helping your kids learn these necessary skills.

Fighting Fairly
Resolving Conflicts Peacefully

"Mom, let's have pizza again. And donuts tomorrow morning."

Brianna is so excited. Tonight she is having a slumber party to celebrate her birthday. For the past three years, she's invited six of her closest friends to sleep at her house. The girls eat pizza and ice cream cake, watch DVDs, and stay awake most of the night – talking and sharing secrets. Brianna looks forward to her birthday party for months and relishes the process of choosing which of her friends she'll invite.

On the other hand, Brianna's mom, Mrs. Harrison, dreads these birthday sleepovers. She has learned from experience that a group of girls hanging out in a small room for long sleepless hours is a recipe for disaster! Mrs. Harrison remembers that last year, two of the girls bickered all night long. The rest of the group, in an effort to smooth things over, spent most of their time and energy mediating between the other two. Every half an hour or so, Brianna reported to her mom about the conflicts in the group. Several times Mrs. Harrison tried to play peacemaker (unsuccessfully) until she was so depleted and exhausted, she fell asleep, leaving the girls to manage their disputes on their own. By morning, the girls were eating donuts as if nothing had happened the night before.

*Every year, Mrs. Harrison vows that she will **never** have another birthday slumber party for Brianna. "Next year," she grumbles to herself, "we'll go out to a movie, and that's it!"*

Fighting is easy; fighting fairly is not. One mistake we make as adults is to assume that kids should be able to resolve their conflicts in an adult manner. The irony is that many adults haven't learned the vital art of compromise. Have you ever heard the expression, "It's her way or the highway"? Developing an effective approach to settling an argument requires self-awareness and self-control. Kids must learn to separate feeling from action, and that they need to give up something in order to get something else. Disputes among peers present a great opportunity for learning this essential life skill.

Conflict between friends provides a unique opportunity for kids to improve their interpersonal relationships. Often, kids don't have the verbal skills to cope effectively with disagreements or the necessary skills to resolve conflicts on their own. As a group leader, you have the chance to teach kids about tolerance and appreciation of diversity in values, ideas, and beliefs. You can also use conflict resolution as a way to help kids express themselves more effectively and clearly. So, welcome the challenge that discord presents. It's a terrific way to help kids grow!

① Know what conflict looks like over time.

Intervention techniques vary depending on the age of the group you are working with, so it's useful to understand what conflict looks like across different age spans. Pre-school kids get upset easily, often, and about seemingly insignificant matters: grabbing of a toy, wanting to be first in line, or getting a smaller piece of cake. Such conflicts are easily resolved with a quick apology and a reassuring hug. Ordinarily, as kids mature, they become less reactive to perceived slights and more able to manage their emotional responses to challenging situations. Whereas tears and temper flair-ups may be a normal occurrence in a pre-school classroom, you would expect to see less of these behaviors in an elementary school classroom.

Although conflicts may diminish in frequency as kids grow older, they do not lessen in intensity. When feelings are not expressed, they fester. Festering generally goes one of two ways: stuffing or exploding. Girls are wonderful stuffers. Boys are terrific exploders. Neither of these conflict resolution styles is particularly effective.

Rather than encouraging girls to express negative feelings directly, our society implicitly supports indirect forms of expression. If unexpressed, however, girls' anger can leak out in unhealthy ways. Notice if the girls in your group are talking behind one another's back, projecting rejecting body language, or using other exclusionary techniques.

Conversely, boys tend to respond to festering by overpowering others either verbally or physically. If boys in your group are behaving in this way, check to see if there is unexpressed anger or unresolved conflict at the root of the problem.

With younger kids, lay the groundwork for future effective communication. In pre-school and early elementary school, teach kids the norms of positive social interaction including taking turns, sharing, playing by the rules, and managing emotions effectively. These basic pro-social behaviors set the stage for the kids to learn more complex social skills later on. Talk with your group about being generous with each other. Point out that sharing and being considerate of feelings makes others feel happy. Reward generous acts with words of praise. Foster empathy in the group. By stressing appropriate social behavior in young children, you're preparing them for successful conflict resolution in their futures.

Resolving Conflicts in Pre-School/Kindergarten

▶ Expect frequent conflicts to occur.

▶ Allow young children to use toys and materials until *they* are ready to pass them on to others.

▶ Encourage empathy (the ability to understand how another person feels) by talking about your own feelings, helping them express theirs, and modeling how they can listen to others.

▶ Reward generous acts, such as sharing and taking turns, with praise.

▶ Minimize competition. Encourage cooperative play instead.

▶ Give kids the opportunity to be both leaders and followers.

▶ Help kids apologize and move on.

▶ Use distraction techniques, such as the "tickle monster," when there is tension brewing.

▶ Encourage kids to express feelings of frustration with words rather than actions.

By the time kids reach elementary school, they are beginning to manage their emotions more effectively. You'll continue to see verbal sparring, but these spats are less frequent and intense. This is the stage when kids are trying to figure out the rules of the game. Fairness becomes all important. Elementary school-age children are less likely to hold a grudge than middle and high school students, but they are becoming more discerning and judgmental about their friendships. You have to resist the urge to use sarcasm to diffuse tension in a group of elementary school kids – they don't understand sarcasm and are insulted by it. Help the kids learn techniques to manage their emotions such as setting up cooling-off zones where kids can go when their emotions are too hot to handle. It is the child who is unable to calm down in the face of intense emotion that we have to worry about. In teenage years, he may become aggressive.

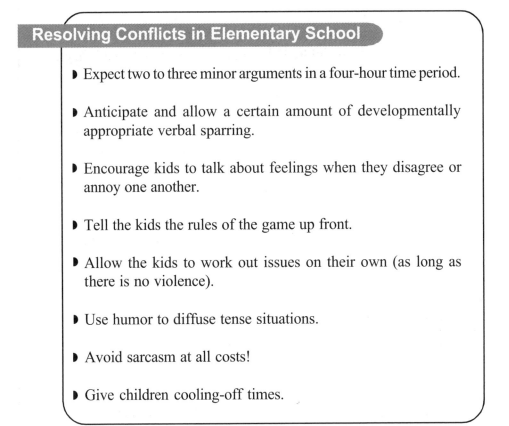

Resolving Conflicts in Elementary School

▶ Expect two to three minor arguments in a four-hour time period.

▶ Anticipate and allow a certain amount of developmentally appropriate verbal sparring.

▶ Encourage kids to talk about feelings when they disagree or annoy one another.

▶ Tell the kids the rules of the game up front.

▶ Allow the kids to work out issues on their own (as long as there is no violence).

▶ Use humor to diffuse tense situations.

▶ Avoid sarcasm at all costs!

▶ Give children cooling-off times.

Teenagers are capable of talking things through successfully, but they may need adult guidance. Higher-level skills like compromise develop during this age. It's essential to emphasize in your group the ability to regulate emotions. It's not enough to tell a group of fighting football players to "Knock it off!" After things cool off, get back together as a group and figure out what happened, how everyone is feeling, why the situation occurred, and what the group can do to fix it.

You'd be surprised how effective it can be to "debrief" with teenagers. After a difficult situation, teens enjoy talking about what happened and how the group could change the experience next time. They also like to compliment each other on interactions that were helpful and supportive. At a summer camp where I recently consulted, the counselors reported that a quick meeting at the end of any activity to review what they did, what went right, and what went wrong, was very helpful in clearing the air for the next group meeting.

Resolving Conflict in Middle School and Beyond

▶ Overt arguing happens less frequently than in grade school.

▶ Don't let conflicts fester. Encourage kids to bring them out into the open.

▶ Offer the kids opportunities to participate in a group problem-solving process.

② Set the stage for minimal conflict.

Have you ever noticed that a cohesive group is a productive and happy one? Take the time and energy to create a situation where everybody belongs. An ounce of prevention will save you a pound of discord in the future.

What Makes a Group Cohesive?

▶ The kids like each other and have a strong sense of belonging.

▶ The kids like what the group is doing.

▶ Being a group member offers some prestige.

▶ Individual group members get their needs met.

▶ Group members share a common goal.

The key is to make membership in the group attractive and rewarding. Kids take pride in being part of a cool group. The cool group members take care of each other. They feel empowered to reach solutions to problems as they arrive.

Provide opportunities for the kids to work together and express their thoughts and feelings. Always begin with a group planning session. This is the best approach for discouraging negative behavior. Goals are much more likely to be accepted and accomplished if members of the group have participated in the decision making. Posting group goals where all of the kids can see them and reviewing the goals regularly also helps the group feel like they are moving together in the same positive direction.

Imagine if Mrs. Harrison, Brianna's mother, had met with the girls before the slumber party began. During this meeting she might have set the stage for positive interaction by asking the girls to buy in to standards of conduct and behavioral expectations at the party. She might have pointed out some of the difficult events of last year's party to short-circuit similar issues arising at this one.

All groups have a beginning, a middle and an end. It is in the first phase that the group establishes a cooperative, trusting atmosphere and develops its goals and rules. This is the best time to set the stage for peaceful resolution of issues as they arise.

Try Saying This:

"I know that this is going to be difficult for some of you, but I need to remind you that it's lights out at 11 p.m. and no talking after midnight. We trust you guys can accept this rule and follow it."

"I know that last year there were problems in our group with getting along that affected everybody. How can we make sure that everybody gets along this year?"

"We are so happy to have you all here. What a great group!"

Promoting a team mentality will help you maintain harmony. At Brianna's birthday party, if Mrs. Harrison notices tensions arising in the group, she might try to distract the girls by suggesting a collaborative group activity to restore the girls' morale. Frequently, group members are relieved to diffuse tension and do something more constructive.

For example, during a recent mediation meeting at my child's school, I noticed the kids were becoming irritable and disengaged from the process. They were beginning to snipe and jab at each other for seemingly no reason. Deciding to shake things up a bit, I jumped up from my seat and began doing jumping jacks, encouraging others to join me. Soon, all of the kids were laughing, joining me in the fun. When we sat back down, they were less cranky and more able to work effectively with each other.

3 Experiment with structure when needed.

Groups that are prone to bickering may have too much free time on their hands. Perhaps an increase in structure or group activity will reduce friction. It only takes a few minutes of organized distraction to disconnect kids from building tension.

Try These Strategies:

▶ Spontaneously, ask your restless students to get out of their seats to play a game of Simon Says.

▶ Out-of-the-blue, ask your group of quarreling teammates to run a relay race with rewards for the best team time.

▶ Invite a birthday party group to take part in a craft activity.

▶ Break a group into pairs and give each pair a project to work on together until tensions in the room have died down.

At Brianna's birthday party, for instance, the girls could prepare dinner and dessert together. Each girl is assigned an essential role. One sets the table, another makes a list of the pizzas the girls want to order, and the rest of them make cookies.

④ Pay attention to the obvious.

If you notice that two kids seem to be drawn to one other and, simultaneously, at each other's throats, separate them. Simple changes in the environment may change the group dynamic from negative to positive. Look for cues that things may be going awry. Often a simple fix will remedy an entrenched problem.

⑤ Foster open lines of communication.

Communication – both verbal and nonverbal – is a back-and-forth dialogue between group members. Effective communication means that the receiver of information correctly interprets the message that the sender intends to communicate. You must open the channels of communication so that all group members are able to express their thoughts and feelings freely to one another and to you. Provide opportunities for group members to openly discuss issues and concerns. If each group member is helped to realize that she has individual, as well as group, responsibilities, it is likely that problems will be resolved successfully. Without such help, kids tend to either evade problems or let them simmer and blow up into aggressive action.

For instance, let's say you observe whisperings of dissatisfaction circling around your group. One of the girls, let's call her Kate, is offended by another girl's, let's call her Rebecca, behavior. Of course, Kate does not tell Rebecca that she is upset. Instead, she tells a third girl, Jane, who tries to show her solidarity with Kate by exhibiting outrage at Rebecca's behavior. Rebecca hears of the gossip and goes to yet another girl, let's call her Emily, for reassurance. And the cycle continues. Do you see the potential for disaster here? This would be a great opportunity to sit down as a group and ask, "Hey, what's going on here? I'm noticing there is grumbling in the group. Let's get everything out in the open and figure out how to resolve this. Okay?" It's important, particularly with a group of girls, to nip this situation in the bud.

As paramount as it is for group members to express themselves openly, they must also learn to listen. Active listening is a skill that requires constant practice, even into adulthood. Promote active listening by encouraging the receiver to communicate back a solid understanding of what's being communicated. This is done by using social skills like reflective listening and perception checking. Make sure you model these active listening skills whenever you communicate with the group. Active listening shows your group that you respect what they have to say, and that promotes positive group interaction. For more on active listening, see chapter L - Let's Talk.

Try Saying This:

"What I heard you say is….." (reflective listening)

"You are feeling pretty discouraged right now. Is that right?" (perception checking and empathy)

"You think that I'm coming down on you too hard." (perception checking)

"You are telling me that you are late for practice because…." (reflective listening)

"I saw a lot of frustration out there today. Let's sit down and talk about what you are feeling." (providing opportunities for discussion/perception checking)

6 Teach successful conflict resolution techniques.

If you want kids to stop fighting, you've got to teach them new skills for resolving conflicts. They need to learn problem-solving skills and socially acceptable alternatives for getting what they want. When given the skills and guidance, kids can make responsible decisions and effectively manage conflict.

Set guidelines for discussion.

Let the group members know that you are there to help them figure out what happened and to find mutually agreed upon solutions. Prepare them by communicating expectations for behavior and the structure for the discussion. Make sure you keep the kids who are involved in the conflict with you, while you soothe and calm them. They can't begin the conflict resolution process until they are settled down.

Kids' Rules of Conduct During Conflict Resolution

▶ Say what you feel without being interrupted by anyone else in the group.

▶ Listen to what others say without interrupting them.

▶ Avoid making things worse by shouting, being mean, or using a nasty tone of voice.

▶ Express your feelings with "I feel" statements like "I feel hurt when you…."

▶ Speak quietly.

Try Saying This:

"We are going to discuss what happened. Let's try to sort things out so that everyone gets some of what they want."

"Remember how these discussions go. Each person will get a chance to speak. We will listen to each one of you until you are finished speaking."

"Jackie, let's try to understand how Amber is feeling right now."

"Remember we are going to work very hard on using our listening skills."

Clarify what happened. Get the facts and the feelings.

Kids must know that all conflicts are a shared problem, and that there are two sides to the story.

Ask "What happened?" in a calm, neutral voice without judgment. Spend time focusing on feelings. You may want to put a time limit on each child so that everyone gets equal time to be heard by the group. Be sure to review not only the "what happened?" but the "why it happened."

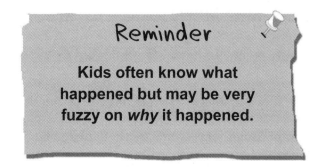

Reminder

Kids often know what happened but may be very fuzzy on *why* it happened.

> **Try Saying This:**
>
> "So what you're saying, Amber, is that you wanted to sit next to Vicki and that it made you mad when Jackie squeezed in between you."
>
> "And what you are saying, Jackie, is that you are feeling frustrated with Amber because you see her as hogging all of Vicki's time and attention."

Analyze the problem by exploring differences in point of view.

Kids need guidance on seeing how their behavior impacts others. In order to generate solutions, they need to become more aware of others' needs.

"Jackie, how do you think Amber felt when you squeezed in next to Vicki?"

"Amber, how do you think Jackie felt when she felt you were hogging all of Vicki's time?"

Help the kids see the ultimate goal for all parties concerned.

Have each child voice the ideal solution, and also what she is willing to let go of. Both kids involved need to see clearly what the other child is giving up before they will be willing to identify possible solutions.

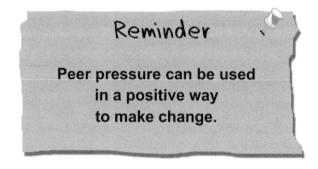

Reminder

**Peer pressure can be used
in a positive way
to make change.**

If a child denies responsibility for her actions, bring the question up to the group for feedback. In this way, peer pressure can be used in a positive manner to help a group member see her part in the conflict.

When you see kids in the group demonstrate active listening skills, let them know it so that others will follow suit. For example, "Kara, I can tell you are really hearing Amber and Jackie's stories. You are looking at them and nodding your head to show them that you are listening."

Generate agreed upon alternative solutions to the problem.

Before solutions can be generated, the group members must develop agreements about the causes of the conflict and the proposed resolutions. Repeat each suggestion as it is offered, and write them down for the group, when possible.

Evaluate the potential consequences of all solutions.

Encourage the kids to voice both the short- and long-term consequences of each solution. Even though you may feel some of the solutions the kids come up with are silly, resist the urge to judge any of them. Judgment kills the spirit and intent of a brainstorming session and defeats the purpose of working together to identify solutions.

Try Saying This:

"What might happen to you if .....?"

"How might Amber feel if you ......?"

"What might happen down the line if you choose to.....?"

Select and implement a solution.

After your group has come up with a good plan, make sure you review the entire process with them. Summarize again what the problem was, reiterate all points of view, and restate the agreed upon solution.

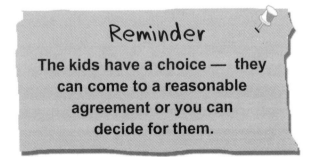

Reminder

The kids have a choice — they can come to a reasonable agreement or you can decide for them.

Praise the group's efforts.

Problem-solving is hard work. Make sure you praise the group for making the effort to resolve the conflict in a healthy way.

Conflict has many negative connotations, evoking images of hurt and violence. You can make an enormous contribution to your group members' lives if you help them learn ways to manage inevitable conflicts as they arise. If you take the steps outlined above, your group will know the skills necessary to create a more peaceful world.

Good Winners/
Good Losers
Improving Sportsmanship

Coach Greg has coached his son Corey's Little League team since Corey began playing five years ago. Greg loves baseball. He played in high school and would have played in college if he hadn't injured his shoulder when he was 17. Corey is a natural athlete and is the team's strongest pitcher, but Greg gets frustrated because Corey doesn't put his "all" into the game. "Corey could win these ballgames for us," Greg thinks, "but he doesn't seem to care whether we win or lose." So Greg rides Corey every second of the game; every time Corey screws up, Greg lets him know it – loudly and clearly. In Greg's mind it's up to Corey to win the game for the team, so he plays Corey even when his son is tired, and the other pitchers haven't played a minute of the game. Greg feels he can't take any chances with one of his weaker pitchers, especially when the score is close.

It's the bottom of the ninth and Coach Greg's team is up by two. There are two outs with two men on base. Corey lets one go and the batter hits a home run. The team loses by one. After the game, Coach Greg tells the team, especially Corey, how upset and disappointed he is in their loss. The team members leave the field feeling dejected and discouraged.

Winning is everything in our society. This "take no prisoners" philosophy pervades the media. Dreadful unsportsmanlike behavior of athletes and coaches in professional sports is condoned. It is not at all surprising that parents and coaches of our youth show a parallel increase in outrageous acts of violence and trash talking. Our kids are influenced by the professionals they idolize. But, more directly, they learn poor sportsmanship from their own parents and leaders.

All too often, coaches choose winning over building character. Competitive sports can offer a unique opportunity to teach kids ethics that can guide them both on and off the field. As a group leader, you have a responsibility to offset the win-at-all-costs approach by instilling in your kids good sportsmanship principles right from the start.

1 Have fun!

Have a "child centered" philosophy. Kids play on teams for two primary reasons: 1) to have fun and 2) to build skills. If you constantly remind yourself to see it from their point of view, you'll be better able to serve their needs, as well as be a more effective coach. As kids grow up and move into more competitive leagues, they become more focused on winning and may forget to have fun. You set the tone for the team. If you have fun, the likelihood is that the kids will have fun, too.

In Coach Greg's situation, Greg's focus on winning deprived his son, as well as the rest of the team, of the thrill of the game. He misinterpreted Corey's enjoyment in just playing as passivity and lack of drive. Greg was so focused on winning that he didn't see that his son was getting tired, and that playing him in the last inning was a set-up for his son's failure.

2 Know yourself well.

Before you can expect your kids to show good sportsmanship, you need to examine how important winning is to you. How much are you willing to sacrifice in order to win? Be honest with yourself. Winning is a "high." It can make you feel like you're a great leader. You feel the kids' success is your success. It's hard to resist the urge to live vicariously through your team's accomplishments.

In Greg's case, Corey's participation in baseball was a way for him to live out some of his own dreams. Greg may have thought that Corey would succeed in baseball in a way that he could not after his shoulder injury. If Greg had been aware of his own motives and reminded himself of his players' needs, he would have made different choices.

Reminder

**Be honest with yourself.
Be aware of whether or not
your kids' winning fulfills
something in you.**

③ Be a role model.

The kids are watching you. If you show respect for your players, the opponents, other coaches, and officials, the children will follow your lead. Gradually, your players will learn that the real winners are those who persevere, learn from their mistakes, and behave with dignity – whether they win or lose. This sounds a whole lot easier than it is. When emotions are high, it's hard to remain level-headed and do the right thing. However, good leaders model good sportsmanship regardless of the circumstances, and make it a core value of their work with teams.

④ Emphasize effort, not outcome.

"It's not whether you win or lose, it's how you play the game" is easier to say than it is to put into practice. The goal is to emphasize the process rather than the final product (the win or the loss). Get in the habit of praising steps in the right direction rather than the end result. For instance, rather than praising the batter when he hits a line drive, commend him for improving his swing.

Greg fell into a common parent coaching trap – he did not treat his own son like he did the rest of the team. His expectations for Corey were unrealistic. Greg may have been focused on improvement in his other players, but his own son did not get the benefit of that positive guidance.

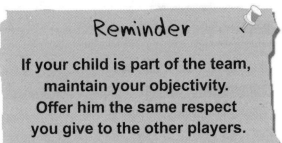

Reminder

If your child is part of the team, maintain your objectivity. Offer him the same respect you give to the other players.

Positive feedback is an excellent way to reinforce skills. Feedback can take the form of suggestions, praise, and support.

Try Saying This:

"Way to keep your eye on that ball!"

"You did a great job bending your knees like we talked about in practice."

"You were really focused out there."

"Good job staying on your toes!"

 Uphold a sportsmanship contract.

Before embarking on competitive play, sit down with your team members and review in detail your expectations for good sportsmanship. Many leaders find it invaluable to create a good sportsmanship pledge at the group's inception. When the players participate in creating their own pledge, they're more likely to adhere to it. If parents are involved, it's not a bad idea to have them sign the agreement too! The pledge should spell out the do's and don'ts of good winning behavior.

Following is a sample pledge with a list of do's and don'ts:

I agree to follow the do's and don'ts of good sportsmanship listed below:

Do's

▶ I *will* congratulate my opponent after each game.

▶ I *will* offer encouragement to all of my teammates (especially the ones who I think are less talented than me).

▶ I *will* play fairly and follow the rules of the game.

▶ I *will* follow the directions of the coach with enthusiasm.

▶ I *will* accept the referee's calls (even when I think he is wrong).

▶ I *will* learn from my mistakes.

▶ I *will* applaud good plays by my teammates as well as my opponents.

▶ I *will* have fun!

Don'ts

▶ I *won't* whine.

▶ I *won't* cheat.

▶ I *won't* criticize my teammates.

▶ I *won't* argue with the referee.

▶ I *won't* "trash talk" my opponents.

▶ I *won't* showboat.

▶ I *won't* quit before the game is over.

▶ I *won't* lose my temper.

▶ I *won't* use profanity.

Player signature: _____

Parent signature: _____

Coach signature: _____

Trust in your team's ability to follow the sportsmanship contract, and verify consistently that they are living up to the agreed-upon guidelines. Before the season begins, establish a strict set of consequences for players who break the contract. For instance, if a kid yells at a referee, he automatically loses playing time in the next game. In some cases, kids need to be suspended from a game for extreme unsportsmanship-like conduct.

Reminder

Begin each game by reviewing the sportsmanship expectations.

6 Don't fall into the parent trap.

Any adult leader will tell you that managing the parents of their kids is much harder than managing the kids themselves. (This topic is covered in more depth in the P – Parents chapter of this book.)

Top Five Parental Behaviors That Can Drive You Crazy!

» Coaching and criticizing kids from the sidelines

» Arguing with referees

» Telling you what to do or criticizing your decisions

» Trash-talking the opposing team

» Losing their tempers and using profanity

Be careful of falling into the trap of caring about other people's opinions (especially parents). Trust yourself and your ability to manage your group objectively. Meet with your kids' parents up front. Share your values and goals with them and give them the opportunity to remove their child from the team if they don't agree with your approach.

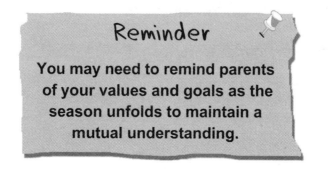

Reminder

You may need to remind parents of your values and goals as the season unfolds to maintain a mutual understanding.

You may want to elect several parent representatives who will gently remind the other parents of the team's goals of good sportsmanship. Parent reps can even wear special T-shirts or pins that visually remind the other parents of the values of the team.

7 Highlight examples of good and bad sportsmanship.

Look for examples of good sportsmanship in professional athletes and point them out to your group members. Talk openly about the bad examples too. Ask the kids what they think of the professional football players who perform a mocking, rub-your-face-in-it dance every time they score a touchdown. Is this an example of "good winning?"

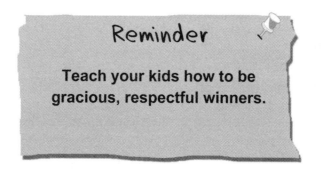

Reminder

Teach your kids how to be gracious, respectful winners.

⑧ Applaud good plays on the other team, too.

Whether the other team is playing well or not, a good sport does not put the opposing team down. Respect for the other team is crucial. Kids have the opportunity to learn from the other team's victories as well as their defeats. Emphasize the great plays made by the other team.

⑨ Offer rewards.

Take note of good sportsmanship behavior. If you see one of your kids helping an opposing player get up after a trip or fall, give them verbal kudos at the end of the game. Jot down a note when you observe players complimenting an opposing team member after a good play, or shaking hands with the referee. All kids like to be praised, especially in front of the team. Highlighting excellent behavior may be enough of its own reward, but you can also reward intermittently with a gift certificate for an ice cream or a slice of pizza as an added incentive.

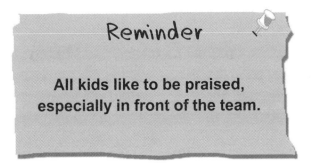

Reminder

All kids like to be praised, especially in front of the team.

⑩ Encourage your players regardless of their performance.

Set a clear expectation with the kids that they should praise and support one another, no matter what happens. Criticizing fellow teammates is unacceptable. As the group leader, you also have a responsibility to encourage the less talented players on the team.

If Greg had put his other pitchers in the game, regardless of their performance level, he would have sent a strong message to his team that the game is not about winning but about having fun and learning to work together.

⑪ Keep winning and losing in perspective.

Even when you and your team are able to keep winning and losing in perspective, there is still going to be disappointment at defeat. Allow yourself and the kids to feel the disappointment that comes with losing. It's only after experiencing these feelings that the team can move on and figure out what lessons to take from the defeat. There is an expression: "The blessings of a skinned knee." A key to learning is going through the process of falling, getting back up, brushing yourself off, and moving forward armed with new information.

Greg's team would have felt less discouraged if he had gently acknowledged the team's loss, but then moved on to talking about lessons learned and future opportunities to succeed.

Hyperactivity
Staying In-Sync with the AD/HD Child

Scott is very pleased with his bunk this year. They seem compatible and he thinks they'll be a fun group. It's gratifying for Scott to see how the boys are responding to him as their counselor, and, after only one week together, he can see that they are becoming a more cohesive group.

However, there is one camper – Ben – who sticks out like a sore thumb. Before his first day of camp, Ben's parents were frank with Scott about Ben's diagnosis of AD/HD (Attention Deficit/Hyperactivity Disorder). They prepared Scott for Ben's challenges. They warned him that as much as Ben loves being at camp, as his medication wears off during the course of the day, he would become increasingly distracted, impulsive, and hyperactive.

Sure enough, Scott notices that Ben has tremendous difficulty focusing on many of the activities after lunch. If the bunk plays an afternoon game of dodge ball, Ben seems distracted by anything and everything – insects on the field, airplanes flying overhead, kids walking by. In addition, he has a very tough time concentrating in arts and crafts and other indoor activities. He fools around, interrupts Scott when he's talking to other kids, and distracts his bunkmates with silly behavior. The other kids react to Ben's "class clown" behavior either by laughing (which only exacerbates his inappropriate behavior) or by becoming annoyed with him.

Scott is at a loss about how to manage Ben's behavior effectively. He finds himself becoming impatient and tempted to yell at Ben, while at the same time he wants to understand and help him become a cooperative camper.

AD/HD is a brain disorder that is commonly associated with certain social behaviors. Kids with AD/HD have trouble paying attention, are easily distracted by external stimulation, and can be behaviorally impulsive. You might think that all boys demonstrate these behaviors to some degree. "Boys will be boys," right? The difference is that the AD/HD child struggles with these behaviors constantly, to the point where it's difficult for him to function normally in social, academic, and home settings. AD/HD kids like Ben are *not* purposely trying to drive others crazy with their provocative behavior. Unfortunately, because many adults don't understand the nature and consequences of AD/HD, they don't understand how to successfully manage the behaviors of a child with the disorder.

Understanding AD/HD Behavior

The child with AD/HD generally exhibits a constellation of characteristics that may interfere with successful social development. These behaviors are even more apparent in groups.

The child with AD/HD is often impulsive.

When a child lacks the adequate pause between impulse and action, social "faux pas" inevitably occur. Poor listening skills are a common byproduct of impulsivity. Because Ben is unable to pause before speaking or acting, he's distracted and fools around during camp activities. His peers and his counselor become annoyed by his constant verbal and nonverbal interruptions.

The child with AD/HD may be insensitive to subtle interpersonal cues.

Being able to recognize and understand other people's body language and facial expressions requires kids to constantly scan their environment for clues that will guide their social actions. Because kids with AD/HD often struggle to stay tuned in to their environments, they frequently misread social signals. Misinterpretations may lead to overreacting to ambiguous social situations. It can also lead to under-reacting. The kids who don't see these signals may be insensitive to the feedback cues (e.g., facial expressions, body language) others are giving them, leading to anger from peers who feel that their "social hints" are being ignored.

When Ben's bunkmates become annoyed with his behavior, he doesn't heed their dirty looks and verbal pleas for him to stop. Ben's AD/HD gets in the way of his being able to learn from the reactions of his peers.

An AD/HD child can't control what captures his attention.

Any internal or external stimulation can be distracting to a child with AD/HD. Because Ben tends to fade in and out of conversations, he frequently misunderstands directions and thus has difficulty following through on instructions accurately.

For instance, when Scott gives Ben specific instructions to do something, Ben seems to be paying attention, but then he goes off to do just the opposite of what Scott suggests. Scott begins to question his own ability to communicate effectively with the youngster.

Children with AD/HD have a hard time learning from experience, whether the experience is positive or negative.

When a non-AD/HD child makes a social mistake and receives a hostile reaction from his peers, chances are high that he won't make that same mistake again. The child with AD/HD, on the other hand, may make a mistake repeatedly before he learns not to do it again. He has trouble applying past experiences to future problems and is unable to predict the consequences of his actions.

In Ben's case, by the time he learn the errors of his ways, his bunkmates are too irritated with him to forgive his past transgressions.

AD/HD children have trouble transitioning from one activity to another.

As hard as it is for the AD/HD child to focus, it can be equally difficult for him to disengage when he is involved in a stimulating activity. Frequently, parents of AD/HD children will say to me, "I didn't think my child was AD/HD for the longest time. How could he be AD/HD when he can play video games for hours and hours without becoming distracted even once!" The difference is that the AD/HD child is just as likely to over-focus on an activity he enjoys as he is to under-focus on one that he can be easily distracted from because it is routine or boring.

Managing AD/HD Kids

If a child with AD/HD is part of your group, you can take the following steps:

1 Accept that AD/HD is a genuine disorder.

Before you can help an AD/HD kid, you must first believe that AD/HD is a genuine brain disorder that results in unintended behaviors and consequences. You need to understand that AD/HD is neither a reflection of a kid's character nor of his intelligence or upbringing. Adults who believe that AD/HD is a made-up diagnosis may think the child's behavior is willful and caused by a lack of discipline or poor parenting. These adults are going to handle their interactions with an AD/HD kid very differently from those who recognize the disorder's impact. It takes a mature, patient, calm adult leader to manage an AD/HD child in a group setting.

2 Focus on positive channeling.

The key to working successfully with the AD/HD kid is to focus on strengths and provide opportunities for learning. AD/HD kids are energizing. They are often passionate, enthusiastic, and active children. Take the time to catch the AD/HD child doing good things, and compliment him! While the standard punishment model of discipline may be appropriate for some kids, it generally backfires with the AD/HD child. Channeling their behavior in a positive manner reduces the odds that misbehavior will occur.

Recently I was asked by a frustrated teacher to observe Aaron, an AD/HD child in her classroom. This AD/HD first-grader had a lot of difficulty staying in his seat during class. It was difficult for the teacher to instruct because Aaron's behavior was so disruptive to the other children. He frequently got up to sharpen his pencil, grabbed pencils off of his classmates' desks, and jumped up to blurt out answers to the teacher's questions. The teacher tried to curtail his behavior by putting him in a seat far away from his peers and sending him to the principal's office when his behavior got out of hand. After my school visit, the teacher and I came up with other ways to help Aaron control himself in class. When she observed that Aaron had "ants in his pants," she would ask him to do active favors for her. For instance, she would ask him to erase the board or go with a buddy to the school office to deliver a message. These activities harnessed some of Aaron's excess energy. After he completed a task, she then could reward him with praise, thus encouraging future positive behavior.

③ Adjust your expectations.

The AD/HD child is approximately two to three years behind his peers in emotional maturity. This can be confusing for adults especially if the AD/HD child is physically large for his chronological age, but behaves several years younger, socially and emotionally.

Adjust your expectations accordingly. In a sports situation, for example, if a typical 12-year-old boy is capable of playing an outfield position during a long inning, recognize that an AD/HD child may not be able to maintain focus for the same amount of time. You might need to change out his position or put in an alternative player if the inning goes on too long.

4 Understand the differences between AD/HD girls and AD/HD boys.

It's important to make a distinction between the social worlds of girls and boys. Boys and girls tend to interact in same-sex groups. They also play very differently from each other. Boys' play tends to involve physical roughhousing and athletic endeavors; girls' play tends to focus on forming friendships and deepening intimacies. Because of these basic differences between boys

and girls, girls are generally even more sensitive to social rejection and neglect than boys.

For the AD/HD child, the above-mentioned characteristics may be common in both sexes but they may surface and get played out quite differently among boys than girls. In addition, male and female peers react differently to AD/HD behaviors. Generally, there's a bit more social rope given to boys than girls. Boys are viewed in society as being more impulsive by nature. Thus, society may turn a blind eye to boys who resolve differences through fighting, for instance. Boys also commonly engage in verbal sparring, thus lending a bit of protection for AD/HD boys such as Ben. In addition, a lot of leeway is given to boys who are gifted athletes. Ben, for example, may be impulsive and troublesome to manage, but if he's good at sports, his counselor, as well as the other kids, would be less inclined to comment on his negative behaviors.

Girls, on the other hand, are generally socialized to be a part of a peer group. Physical prowess is not deemed as important; social savvy is highly stressed, and the challenges AD/HD girls face in a social setting are unique. A girl who's verbally or physically impulsive is not as readily accepted by her peers. Girls exhibiting AD/HD traits are more often rejected and excluded by their female peers than boys with AD/HD.

Once a kid has earned a negative social reputation within the group, it's very difficult to help him undo the damage. It can be accomplished, but the work is slow. It's up to you, as the adult leader, to understand fully what may have contributed to the AD/HD child's poor social reputation, and to help the youngster understand which behaviors he exhibited that turned off other kids.

⑤ Give one-step directions.

Many kids with AD/HD have trouble following multi-step directions. It may be fine for you to tell most kids to make their beds, sweep the floor around their bunk, and hang up their wet towels after swimming. However, if you give the same set of instructions to an AD/HD kid, he might remember to make his bed, but will most likely get distracted and forget the rest of what he was supposed to do.

Reminder

**Give AD/HD kids
directions one step
at a time!**

⑥ React calmly.

Because AD/HD is a disorder of self-control, AD/HD kids may do and say things that they don't mean. Their impulsivity results in their inability to hold their tongues and restrain their actions. It takes a strong adult to refrain from taking the bait and retaliating with punishments and reprimands.

Remain as calm as possible when a child requires correction. Try these strategies:

Correction Strategies

▶ **Encourage rather than criticize.**

"When you are in position, you catch the ball every time!" rather than, "How many times do I have to tell you to stay in your position?"

▶ **Tell them what you want them to do (not just what not to do).**

"Hang your wet towel on this hook," rather than, "Don't throw your wet towel on the floor!"

▶ **Refrain from accusations.**

"It might be better if you tried it this way," rather than, "You are doing it all wrong!"

▶ **Catch the child exhibiting positive behavior.**

"I really liked how you helped out your bunk mate!"

▶ **Shape behavior through praise.**

"Wow. That was a great throw to first base!"

7 Ask about the parents' method of discipline.

Scott is lucky that Ben's parents trusted him enough to let him know about Ben's AD/HD. Frequently, parents of AD/HD children are reluctant to let adult leaders in on their child's condition for fear that the child will be judged and ostracized. By giving Scott a heads-up about Ben's likely behavior after his medication wears off, they were enabling Scott to manage Ben more effectively. Ben's parents know him best. Over the years, they have developed ways to deal with his behavior successfully. Scott benefits from getting as much information from them as he can.

▶ What would you like me to do to encourage good behavior?

▶ What disciplinary methods do you use at home that you find effective?

▶ What can I do to help motivate your child?

 Help the AD/HD child "switch gears" slowly.

You can help an AD/HD child shift activities by preparing them to make a transition. AD/HD kids respond very well to predictability and structure, so they appreciate knowing the routine. Rather than expecting an AD/HD kid to do something "NOW!" it's best to give them time to prepare to switch gears.

Try Saying This:

"Okay, guys, in three minutes, we're getting our suits on to go the pool."

"Ben, are you finished with your craft project? It's almost time to wrap up."

"Five more minutes before we have lights out." (Two minutes later.) "Okay, time to turn off the lights." (One minute later.) "Is everyone in bed with the lights out?"

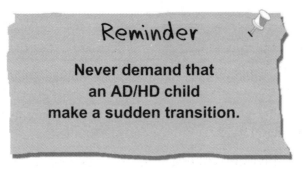

⑨ Redirect whenever possible.

Some AD/HD children move around a lot. They will fidget with anything close by. This can be distracting to others when the objects are large or noisy, but this can actually be useful in harnessing the AD/HD kid's energy. For example, giving an AD/HD kid a rubber ball to squeeze, a rubber-ended pencil to chew on, or worry beads can help him stay busy and tuned in to those around him. If you supply the object yourself, it is less likely to be something that will distract the entire group!

When an AD/HD kid is over-stimulated, he may become revved up and more difficult to control. This is when the "redirecting" technique comes in handy. Rather than admonishing, redirecting captures the child's attention and allows him time to refocus and settle down.

To cope with troublesome, distracting behavior, try these ideas:

Dealing with Distracting Behavior

▶ **Change your proximity to the AD/HD kid.** Sometimes simply moving closer to him will do the trick.

▶ **Call the AD/HD child's attention to something else.** For example, "Hey, Ben, I think there is a ball out on the field. Can you pick it up for me?"

▶ **If the child becomes defiant, ask him to do simple favors for you and praise his immediate attention to your request.** For example, "Ben, would you please go and collect all of the bats for me? Hey, thanks for getting those right away. You're a big help!"

▶ **If the child is "on a roll" of negative behavior, send him on a "non-punitive" time-out by asking him to do an errand for you.** For example, "Ben, could you run over and ask the counselor from the bunk next door for a light bulb? I noticed ours is burned out."

It requires a good deal of effort to be a positive mentor and leader to an AD/HD child. AD/HD kids already receive a lot of negative attention and criticism, so it's very important that they do not receive more of it from you. If you feel that you're going to lose your patience and say or do something that might be hurtful, take some space for yourself. A self-imposed break from the situation may give you just the few moments you need to think clearly about how to respond in a calm, cool-headed fashion.

Icebreakers
Setting the Stage for Progress

It's the first day of a week-long adventure day camp. Rick is a little nervous. This is his first experience as a camp counselor, and he wants his campers to have a rewarding and memorable week. Rick has some questions before he begins: "How can I help a group of excited kids get to know each other quickly? Knowing that building friendships is a major goal of this experience, how can I promote relationships within the group? Many of the kids are just as anxious as I am. How can I, as the leader, help break the ice with my kids?"

The getting-to-know-you phase of any group is crucial to laying the groundwork for future positive relationships to be developed within the group. Icebreakers are a useful way to establish rapport between the kids in order to create a level of safety and support that is necessary for a group to function with a sense of purpose.

The following is a list of pointers to help your icebreaker activities go smoothly:

Icebreaker Tips

▶ **Be enthusiastic! Enjoy yourself!**

▶ **Learn group members' names quickly.**

▶ **Communicate that each member is important, accepted, and secure.**

▶ **Know your audience.** Before you choose your icebreaker exercises, find out if any of the children already know one another. Also determine the group's cognitive, emotional, and physical capabilities.

▶ **Create an atmosphere that is safe and nonjudgmental.**

▶ **Be flexible and spontaneous.** If you don't think the game is working, be prepared to change it at a moment's notice.

▶ **Don't worry about all the "bells and whistles."** You will notice that many of these games require no props at all. You don't need fancy toys to have a great time with your group.

▶ **Keep it simple**. Remember, you want to get to know your kids, and you want them to get to know each other. This will happen if you encourage simple sharing and communication.

Icebreaker Exercises

Although there are hundreds of icebreakers to choose from, I will suggest to you the ones that I have found beneficial in my work with children in our *Stepping Stones* social skills training program. We always begin new sessions with a set of icebreaker exercises. I suggest you read through all of the exercises below, and pick out the ones that feel right for you and for your group. You'll also find that some activities may be appropriate for either younger or older children.

Icebreakers for Younger Children

Roll the Ball
Equipment: Kickball

Ask the kids to sit in a circle. Begin by rolling the ball to one child, who catches it and then says his name and something about himself. That child then rolls the ball to another child in the circle, who does the same thing. This is a gentle, easy way for the kids to get to know one another.

Passing the Eyes Game

Ask the kids to sit in a circle. Begin by making direct, sustained eye contact with the child to your left. Then they pass the eye contact, also direct and sustained, to the child to their left. You can make it a little more challenging by letting the children "pass the eyes" to anyone in the circle. This game helps the kids learn the importance of good eye contact.

Group Drawing
Equipment: Large white paper, colored markers

Each child takes a turn drawing part of a group picture. While one child draws, the child next to him describes what is being drawn. The other kids pay attention quietly. Give everyone a different colored marker so they can easily recognize which part of the picture they drew. After everyone has had a chance to draw, take turns asking each child to describe the part of the picture he created.

Koosh Ball Name Game
Equipment: One Koosh ball

The kids sit in a circle facing one another. Have one child call out the name of another child in the circle, and toss the Koosh ball to him. Then that second child calls out another child's name and tosses the Koosh ball to that third child. This is repeated until all the kids have been included. This helps kids learn each other's names right off the bat.

Animal Nicknames

While sitting in a circle, all the kids think of an animal that starts with the first letter of their first name, e.g., "Raccoon

Rich," "Elephant Evan." Then, each child introduces himself by his animal nickname and repeats the animal nickname of each child who preceded them. Continue until all of the kids have had a turn.

Pop-Up

This is a great first game to play with a group of little ones. Ask the children to pop up from their seats each time they agree with a statement made by the leader, such as, "I have blue eyes," "I like to play soccer," "My favorite subject is math." The kids enjoy seeing how much they have in common with others in the group.

The Story Game

Sit in a circle. Begin making up a story. Stop after a few sentences and ask the child on your left to continue the story. It's important that each child waits his turn before speaking. Ask the kids to connect their part of the story to the parts that preceded it.

Indoor Icebreakers for All Ages

Pair Up

Divide the kids into pairs. Give them fifteen minutes to get to know each other. During that time, they are required to learn two new pieces of information about their partner. Then everyone returns to the main group to report on what they've discovered.

Human Tangle

Instruct the kids to stand in a circle, shoulder to shoulder. Have them put both their arms in the center of the circle and hold hands with two people across from them. Make sure that everyone is holding the hands of two different people and is not holding hands with the person next to them. Keeping all hands held together, the group needs to work as a team, and use decision making and problem-solving skills to try to get untangled.

The Puzzle Hunt
Equipment: Magazines, postcards, scissors

(This game is easier to do in small groups.) Prepare a jigsaw puzzle for each player by cutting magazines and postcards into pieces. Hide all but one piece of each puzzle in the room. Give each child a single puzzle piece. All of the kids must help one another find all of the missing pieces and put all the puzzles back together.

Blanket Ball
Equipment: One blanket

Ask the kids to hold each end of a blanket so that it lays flat between them. Place a large, lightweight ball in the middle of the blanket. The group's goal is to figure out how to cooperatively move the blanket up and down in order to toss the ball into a nearby basket or trash can.

The Alligator Pond
Equipment: Two long wooden boards

The group uses two wooden boards as a "bridge" to get from the start position to the finish position. Everyone has to walk across the bridge. If someone falls off, they get "eaten" by the alligator, and the whole group must return to the start position and begin again. Encourage the kids to concentrate on working together, and to brainstorm ways to stay on the board without falling.

Stare

Divide the group into pairs. Ask the children to line up shoulder to shoulder facing their partner. The children are given one minute to stare at their partners. The goal is to take in every aspect of their partner's appearance. Then, ask the kids to turn and face away from their partner. The kids have 10 seconds to change something about their appearance, such as taking off a shoe, pulling up a collar, changing a ring to another finger, etc. The change needs to be subtle, but visible. Then the players turn back to face each other. They have 30 seconds to discover the change!

Nametag Switch

Equipment: Nametags and a pen

This game is a great way to get to know everyone's name. Give each person someone else's nametag and tell the group to figure out which nametag goes with which person.

Cooperative Musical Chairs

In this version of musical chairs, no one is eliminated. Instead, kids who can't find a chair when the music stops have to share a chair with another child. (Make sure you model how to "gently" sit on someone's lap.) Have the group pick a song to sing and ask everyone to start by marching around the chairs. When you signal the singing to stop, everyone has to find a place to sit down. Randomly pick some letters of the alphabet and have the people whose names start with those letters remove their chairs, and sing another song. Keep removing chairs until you have lots of kids sitting on other kids' laps!

"Are You My Friend?"

Group members arrange their chairs in a circle. One person is selected to be the first "friend." This player does not have a chair and moves into the middle of the circle so there is always one fewer chair than there are group members. The friend chooses one of the players sitting in a chair and greets him with a handshake and the question, "Are you my friend?" The person in the chair must answer, "Yes, I'm your friend, and I like people who _____." (At this point the sitting player uses their imagination to identify some characteristics that several or all of the other players have such as, "have brown hair," or "play on a soccer team.") Now, all members (including the member in the center) possessing this named attribute have to get up and find a different chair to sit in. (No pushing or shoving is allowed.) The person left standing becomes the next "friend." Children can only be in the center once.

Name That Tune

Equipment: Paper and pen

Each person in the group is given a piece of paper with the name of a song written on it (e.g., Twinkle Twinkle, Jingle

Bells, etc.). Each player sings the song that appears on their paper. They must then find everyone else who may be singing the same song. Those with the same songs join together in groups and sing in unison.

"Yankee Swap" Gift Exchange
Equipment: Items from home

Ask each person to bring in something from home that means something special to him, and that he is willing to part with (nothing worth a lot of money). Place the items in the center of the group. One at a time, each member takes something (not the item he brought) from the center and tells why he is attracted to that object. Then, the group member who brought the item tells why it is special to him. This is a great opportunity for sharing and developing camaraderie. (Ideas for what kids can bring: stuffed animals, books, trading cards, dolls, etc.)

Statue

This is a great game for getting the kids to settle down if they are rowdy. Have everyone form a circle. You, as leader, start by standing in the middle and striking a statue pose. Have the kids imitate your pose. They must be silent while doing so. Take turns going around the circle with each child modeling their own statue pose.

Mirror, Mirror on the Wall

You can play this two ways – in partners or as a group. With partners, one person is the mirror and the other person performs the actions. The mirror person has to reflect exactly what the performer does. Then, reverse roles. To play with the entire group, have one person perform the actions while the rest of the group reflects back as mirrors.

Improvisation

Whisper the description of a scene to two group members, giving each player a role to play in the scene. Ask them to act out the scene for a few minutes. Then, ask another group member to enter the scene and change it. This player taps the shoulder of one of the people in the scene. That player must remove himself from the scene. The remaining player must then "go with the flow" and begin acting out the new player's scene.

Shoe Biz

Have the group stand in a circle. Everyone places both of their shoes in the center. Ask the group members to chose two different shoes (that are not their own) and put them on (regardless of whether or not they fit). The group then needs to match the shoes by standing next to the person who is wearing the other show. This results in a bit of chaos and lots of laughs.

Freeze Frame

Let the kids know that this game requires a lot of restraint. Divide the group into pairs, facing away from each other. Explain to the group that at the count of three, they are to face their partner, and stare at one another without smiling, laughing, or talking. Players who smile, talk, or laugh are out, and the remaining players have to find a new partner. When there is one person left standing, all of the kids try to heckle this person to get them to smile.

Candy Game
Equipment: M & M's or other candy

(Make sure no one in the group has an allergy to nuts.) (Also, if anyone knows the game, ask them not to give it away.) Have a supply of M & M's to share with the group. Ask the group to sit in a circle. Pass the M & M's around and ask each member to take as many as he needs. Don't tell the kids what they'll need the candy for. You'll notice that some of the kids will take a few, and some will take *a lot*! Then, ask the group members to state out loud a personal strength for each M&M they took.

Wink
Equipment: A deck of cards

This game can be played with a deck of cards, or without one. If you play without cards, the group stands or sits in a circle.

Begin by telling the kids to close their eyes. While their eyes are closed, squeeze one of the kids' shoulders, designating him "the winker." The goal of the winker is to eliminate everyone in the group before anyone realizes that he is the winker. Now, ask the group to stare at each other. While they are doing this, the winker winks subtly at one player. Five seconds later, that player pretends to die. (The more outrageously performed the death scene, the better!) When someone thinks they know who the winker is, they can guess. If they're wrong, then both the guesser and the wrongly accused winker must "die."

If you play with cards, use only as many cards as there are players (and make sure one of them is the Queen of Spades). All players draw cards. The player who chooses the Queen of Spades is the murderer/winker. Proceed with the game as above.

Truth, Truth, Lie

Ask the kids to think of two things about themselves that are true, and one thing that is a lie. Each person shares those three things about themselves with the rest of the kids. The group must figure out which is the lie. Sometimes the truths are more unbelievable than the lies!

My Grandmother's Trunk

This icebreaker can be played with many variations. The group forms a circle. The first person says his name and something about himself, such as, "My name is Jesse, and I am a swimmer." The group continues on to the next person who must repeat the names and the information of all the group members that came before: "His name is Jesse, and he is a swimmer. My name is Matt, and my favorite food is spaghetti," and so on. This is a very challenging game, particularly for the last person in a large group.

Another variation of this game is to have the first person say, "My grandmother went on a trip. In her trunk, she took a " _____ " (name an object). Then continue as above.

Who Am I?

Equipment: Paper, pen, tape

You may recognize this one as a popular party game. In this exercise, group members are asked to figure out who they are. You tape the name of a famous person on each participant's back. Everyone mills about the room asking "yes" or "no" questions of each famous person until they figure out who they are. If a player receives a "yes" answer, he can continue to ask that person questions. If he receives a "no" response, he must move on to someone else. The exercise finishes after everyone in the group has figured out who they are.

The TV Talk Show Host Game

All the kids in the group divide into pairs and interview each other as if they were on a TV talk show. If you can videotape the talk show game so the kids can see it later, that's even better. The host of the talk show has three goals:

1. Help make your guest feel more comfortable.

2. Ask questions of your guest that show interest.

3. Share information about yourself that relates to your guest's topic.

The guest has three goals:

1. Answer the host's questions politely and appropriately.

2. Stay focused on the topic.

3. Listen when the host is speaking.

Ask the kids to swap roles so they can experience both sides.

Outdoor Games for All Ages

Rolling Logs

Pair children up and have them lay on their backs on the ground. Their feet should touch each other so that they look like one long log. The idea is to have them roll over in unison, without having their feet come apart. Ask them to roll over two, three, four times in a row. Change partners and repeat. Next try making a log by crossing legs and arms. Or make longer logs by having two players lay down and touch their feet and another player lay down and touch hands. Keep adding kids to the log until the whole group is attached.

Over, Under, and Around Kick Ball
Equipment: Kickball

This one is great for teamwork! First set up a long, straight boundary line. Divide the kids into two groups. Have one team scatter themselves across the playing field. The other team will form a straight line about three feet back from, and parallel to, the boundary line. The first person in line gets to kick first and the kicker may kick the ball anywhere in front of the boundary line. The team in the field runs over to the location where the ball was kicked. Then they form a line and the first person in line passes the ball over his head to the next player, who passes it under his legs to the next player, who passes it over his head, then under, and so forth, until everyone on the field has touched the ball in this sequential pattern. When the last player in line receives the ball, the team in the field yells, "Stop!" While all the commotion is happening in the field, the kicker is busy trying to score points by running circles around his team of players, who are standing in line. The kicking team chants a score each time the player finishes running around the whole team. An inning is over when everyone has had a chance to kick.

Amoeba Tag

Two kids are tagged "it." They hold hands and chase the other group members. Each person they catch joins the chain by linking hands. When another person is caught, the chain can stay together or split into another pair. When a chain splits, it must split into an even numbered chain. The game is played until nobody is left running freely.

Dragon Tag

Everyone links hands together in a line. Designate a head and a tail. The object of the game is for the head to catch the tail.

Slow Motion Tag

Ask all of the children to move in slow motion. Call out body parts that must be tagged in slow motion, e.g., feet, elbows, knees.

Little Chickens Come Home

One person is chosen to be the mama hen. Everyone else stands on one side of the field. (Outside boundaries of the field are clearly defined.) The mama hen stands in the middle of the field and says, "Little chickens come home." Everyone yells "No!" (Repeat again.) The mama hen says, "Little chickens come home right now!" Everyone tries to run to the other side of the field without getting tagged by the mama hen. Anyone who gets tagged has to help the mama hen until there is only one chicken left.

Big Ball

Equipment: Large exercise ball, beanbags, Koosh balls

Divide the group into two teams. Place the teams on opposite sides of the field. Divide up the balls and beanbags equally. Put the large ball in the middle. When the leader says, "Go!" the teams begin throwing the smaller balls at the big ball. The object is to move the large ball to the other side of the field.

Clean Up Your Room

Equipment: Beanbags, Koosh balls, scarves, other objects

Divide into two teams and split the equipment equally between the teams. Make a middle boundary line. Tell the kids to start throwing objects to the other side of the boundary line when you say, "Go!" When you stop the game, see who has the "cleanest room." Ask the group members to decide which team has the cleanest room.

Try This: Give Your Group a Name!

Children love having a group identity. Ask the kids to come up with a group name and then have them draw a group mural together that reflects the name they have chosen, such as "The Thunderbirds" or the "The Rocket Ships." Hang the mural in a prominent place for all to see. Refer to the group by its name as often as you can. This encourages teamwork and group solidarity.

Be creative and design your own variations of the activities outlined above. I'll give you an example of leader ingenuity. Recently, YMCA Camp Kern in Ohio piloted a friendship building project using many of the activities from this chapter. This talented group of counselors expanded upon the basic ideas to create exciting new games that were a big hit at camp. Using the "Roll the Ball" game, for instance, the counselors asked their campers to come up with questions that they could write all over a big beach ball. There were questions like, "How did you get your first scar?" and "Where is your favorite place to hide?" When the ball was rolled to a camper, wherever his left pinkie was touching a question on the ball, that was the question that had to be answered. The campers loved not only coming up with their own questions, but also getting to know each other in this fun, inventive way. This is a great example of how you can make this chapter's activities work for your particular group. Don't be afraid to experiment and try new approaches and ideas. You can always discard what doesn't work. Above else, have fun and start your group off on the right foot with icebreakers!

Jealousy
Soothing the Green-Eyed Monster

Maria and Erin have been best friends since the third grade. Now, in the ninth grade, the girls still like to engage in a lot of the same activities. Both girls play soccer in the spring and swim in the winter. They both like to go shopping, to hang out at the mall with their friends, and to have sleepovers together. Erin is Maria's best and only close friend. She doesn't hang out with any other girls, and when Erin is not available, Maria stays home and watches TV. Erin, on the other hand, has a lot of different friends. She has close relationships with girls on the swim team, in her church youth group, and from her sleep-away camp. Erin has no difficulty balancing all of her relationships. There is only one problem: Maria! Maria can't stand it when Erin hangs out with anyone else. When Maria learns that Erin went out with another friend and didn't invite her, she becomes enraged with Erin. At best, she gives Erin the cold shoulder; at worst, she whines and cries to Erin about how left out she feels when she's not included.

What makes matters worse is that the scenes between the girls make everyone around them uncomfortable. During Maria's bouts of jealousy, the tension between them affects their fellow teammates as well as their class-mates. During one of these episodes, the girls are either fighting or loudly ignoring each other. Other girls get pulled into the conflict which only increases the tensions in the group. Their soccer and swim coaches and their teachers don't know what to do or say to turn their behavior around.

Jealousy refers to the thoughts, feelings, and behaviors that occur when a person believes a valued relationship is being threatened. Jealousy usually

involves anger and possessiveness. Sometimes, jealousy is mistakenly confused with envy; however, they are not the same thing. Envy is a regretful longing for something someone else has. For example, when you wish that you could afford the same kind of vacations to the Caribbean that your best friend takes three times each winter, you are envious, not jealous. When you wish that your loved one only paid attention to you because you become enraged whenever he pays attention to someone else, that's jealousy!

We all feel jealousy from time to time; it's a normal human emotion. It's when jealous feelings are not kept in check that they become destructive. Regardless of whether a relationship is platonic or intimate, when one person in the relationship experiences jealousy, it is a signal that something in the relationship needs to be fixed.

Kids maintain complex social systems in which their peers play diverse roles. One person within a social network is a close intimate while another is only an acquaintance. A teammate is a buddy on the field, but not off. A lunch mate is sought after in the cafeteria, but never phoned outside of school. A kid may feel closer to one friend in the social group than to another. This complicated network functions well when all the kids are in agreement about each other's roles. However, it becomes thorny when the kids are not in agreement.

Most children can handle the frustrations associated with sharing friends. But there are some children who have enormous difficulties navigating these waters. Kids who are lonely or have low self-esteem often do not have the skills to handle the risks associated with sharing friends with others. They are the most prone to feeling threatened and vulnerable in their relationships with peers.

In general, girls are more prone to jealousy in friendships than are boys, perhaps because they have higher expectations for loyalty, commitment, and empathy from their friends. It's also more socially acceptable for boys to express jealousy within their intimate relationships. Here, jealousy is seen as a masculine expression of love rather than a sign of insecurity and low self-esteem.

In Maria and Erin's case, Maria's jealousy not only affects her relationship with Erin, it also impacts her relationships with the rest of their social group. While her desire to protect her friendship with Erin is understandable, Maria's extreme displays of aggressive and passive-aggressive behavior are destructive. Both Erin and the group as a whole are tired of Maria's negative behavior.

How to Handle Jealousy in Your Group

So what's a leader to do? The impact of inappropriate jealousy on a group can be toxic. This is clearly the case with Maria and Erin. Here are some strategies their coaches and teachers can use to restore the peace:

⓵ Give each girl time to talk to you alone.

Kids need time to share their feelings with an objective person, especially during times of stress. They are no different from adults in this way. They don't want to hear advice or long lectures or even the other person's point of view. They just want someone to acknowledge their feelings and give them a chance to talk, without being judged.

② Show that you understand the feelings behind the words.

Kind statements that acknowledge feelings give a child comfort and allow effective problem solving to take place. It may sound simple just to make a statement that shows you understand the feelings of the child. But it's not. When a child is pouring her heart out to you, only through practice and concentration are you able to see behind the words to identify the feelings.

Try Saying This:

"To have a friend go out with other friends and not invite you can really hurt."

"You're really angry about this."

"You feel the whole group is against you."

③ It's okay to feel jealous.

Acknowledge that jealousy is a normal human emotion that everyone feels from time to time. Empathize with the feelings of insecurity beneath the jealousy.

Try Saying This:

"No one likes to feel they may be losing a friend."

"You may be worried that Erin prefers other friends to you."

"Sometimes when we feel insecure in a relationship, it makes us want to hold on even tighter."

4 Resist the temptation to solve the problem.

Resist the urge to fix the problem. Kids can learn critical life skills through figuring out how to manage difficult situations like these.

In a parent group I was leading recently, a mom described her frustrations with her twelve-year-old son's jealous feelings about his best friend's friendship with another boy. In an effort to regain the friend's attention, her son engaged in inappropriate behavior, driving the friend even further away. This mother's impulse was to chastise her son for his behavior, but she was able to start empathizing with him, listening without judgment while he figured out his own strategy for coping with this difficult situation. After thinking through his options, her son made some positive choices to handle his feelings. Mom's neutrality allowed her son to solve his problem successfully. When you listen to children supportively, frequently they can figure it out for themselves and make good decisions.

5 Support efforts to talk openly with each other.

In general, girls are not socialized to be direct in getting what they need from their relationships. That's why it's important to support their efforts to talk openly with each other about their fears regarding friendships. Maria and Erin could start by talking with each other about what is bothering each of them in the friendship. Encourage them to sit down and figure out some solutions to their issues. This type of conversation is best held away from the rest of the group. The dynamics among different group members around alliances and power only serve to enhance the drama. If a conflict is between just two group members, it is best to let them work it out on their own.

6 Encourage the recipient of unhealthy jealousy to set clear limits with the other person.

In Erin and Maria's situation, support Erin in being direct with Maria, and encourage her to describe those jealous behaviors that are unacceptable to her.

Erin Could Try Saying This:

"It is not okay to call my house over and over when I'm out. If you do that again, I will not call you back."

"I don't like it when you yell at me in public. Next time you are upset, I'll talk to you, but only if we can do it privately."

"It is hurtful to me when you snub me. If you have something to say to me, please say it directly."

You can see that many of these statements would also work well for romantic jealousy. Frequently, the object of the jealousy tries to appease rather than set limits on their romantic partner's behavior.

7 Meet with the two friends together.

If the jealousy continues after the above steps are taken, consider meeting with the two friends together to help them talk things through. Treat the meeting like a mediation session, using your conflict resolution skills to help the kids come up with an agreement that is acceptable to both parties.

Mediation Process

▶ Make sure that both parties willingly agree to meet.

▶ Ask each child to tell her side of the story, in full, without interruption.

▶ Listen and reflect on all feelings equally. Stay neutral!

▶ Show that you understand each kid's perspective by making statements such as, "Are you saying…." and "It sounds like you are feeling…."

Mediation Process (cont'd)

▶ Brainstorm solutions. All solutions are treated with respect.

▶ Look for areas of agreement and present possible solutions that are comfortable for both parties.

▶ Decide together which solutions to try first.

▶ Clarify the first step that needs to be taken toward achieving successful resolution, i.e., who will do what and when.

▶ Write down a clear plan.

▶ Ask each person to sign the agreement.

▶ Meet again to discuss how the plan is working.

---

8 Express your concern to the parents.

You may not need to involve parents if the jealous interactions are rare and mild in nature. When the jealousy is ongoing, intense, and pervasive, however, it is important to communicate your concerns to both sets of parents, separately. Let them know the steps you have taken to resolve the problems. Ask for their help.

Make concrete observations about each child's behavior. When you see red flags indicating an unhealthy relationship, write them down.

Example - Leader observations of Erin:

▶ Seems afraid to talk to peers because of how Maria will react

▶ Apologizes to Maria continuously

▶ Is withdrawing from the others in group

Example - Leader observations of Maria:

▶ Yells at Erin in front of the group

▶ Angrily sulks for days on end

▶ Controls Erin's behavior by threatening to end their relationship

9 If jealous behavior escalates, refer the kids for professional help.

Kids with low self-esteem are more prone to jealousy. They tend to worry so much about their relationships that they are unable to enjoy them. They approach their friendships with a high level of distrust that can leave them feeling lonely and at risk for depression. The following list contains signs that jealous behaviors are escalating to an unhealthy level. Here are some questions to ask to elicit responses that will help you decide if jealousy has gone too far and professional help is indicated.

Signs that Jealousy Is Going Too Far

Does your friend do any of the following?

▶ Flies into possessive rages

▶ Ignores you for days when you've gone out with another friend

▶ Calls your cell phone to check up on your whereabouts

▶ Follows you and turns up out of the blue

▶ Interrogates your other friends and family about you

▶ Eavesdrops on your conversations

Signs that Jealousy Is Going Too Far (cont'd)

▶ Hangs out in your house when you aren't around

▶ Has to know where you are at all times

▶ Tries to control you by telling you what to do

▶ Tries to isolate you from your family and friends

If you observe these behaviors, it's best to refer the child to a professional. These kids need to work on understanding their underlying insecurities and learning to express feelings and needs appropriately. Whether through group therapy or one-on-one counseling, kids can learn how to monitor negative thoughts and replace them with more positive ones. They are encouraged to talk about their feelings and develop constructive ways to cope with them. In this manner, kids learn that they need to process thoughts and feelings before acting, and this increased awareness leads to necessary changes in behavior.

⑩ Teach the kids what healthy relationships look like.

Remind the kids that you are there for them and available to talk if they need you. Teach them how important respect and communication are in developing healthy relationships with friends and loved ones. Friendship is a mutual relationship formed with affection and commitment between people who consider themselves equals.

Keeping Kids' Secrets
A Closer Look at Confidentiality

The whole cheerleading squad is worried about Ashley. For the last six months, when the girls go to McDonald's for a snack after practice, Ashley gorges herself on junk food. Sometimes she eats two Big Macs and a large fries at one sitting. After she finishes eating, she goes to the bathroom and returns with bloodshot eyes and really bad breath. When the girls ask Ashley what she's doing in the bathroom, she reveals that she's been throwing up, but makes all of them promise not to tell anyone. The girls agree, except that one of them, Nina, feels torn about it. She's worried that Ashley is hurting herself and needs help, but she doesn't want to tell anyone else because she knows Ashley and the rest of the squad will come down on her for telling. Eventually, Nina can't take the pressure any more, and she goes to meet secretly with the squad leader, Ms. King. "Please, Ms. King," Nina pleads. "You can't tell anyone. I have to tell you a secret."

We typically think of secrets as barriers to honest, open communication between people. However, not all secrets fall into that category. For kids, secrecy actually plays a significant role in the development of their identity. Because they still see their parents as omnipotent, very young children have doubts about keeping secrets. They're comfortable responding openly when asked personal questions, so keeping secrets is challenging for them. As they get older, however, kids begin to see secrecy as intricately tied in with friendship. In early adolescence, children come to realize that keeping a friend's secret is of absolute importance, and to betray a peer's confidence can mean losing a friend. Teenagers see themselves as trusted keepers of their friends' secrets. The more illicit the content of the secret, the more valued the friend is who can keep silent about it.

During the teen years, the natural move toward peers and away from family is underscored when secrets are kept from parents. Keeping secrets requires certain skills that develop at this age, such as self-control and personal choice. No longer is the child an open book, wanting to express every thought and feeling to the all-powerful parent. Now, she feels protective of the private world belonging to her and her friends. Parents feel shut out. The teenager gains a sense of power by holding on to information that's off-limits  to parents. These are the years when adolescents are learning to look inward and develop a deeper sense of self. In this sense, keeping secrets from parents is a sign of growth toward independence and emotional autonomy.

When a child, particularly a teenager, confides in you, she is telling you that she has deep faith in you – it is a strong statement about the strength of your relationship. In a majority of cases, you will be able to keep her confidences. However, there are secrets that are not meant to be kept. Trust your gut feelings on this. If the secret you are being asked to keep makes you feel uncomfortable, nervous, or frightened, it is probably a "bad secret" that should not be kept a secret.

Bad secrets may be expressed openly to you. They may also be expressed nonverbally. A good leader is perceptive. Keep your eyes open for signs of trouble. Acknowledging that destructive secrets exist is a first step toward addressing the issues behind the secret.

Carrie, a teenage girl in one of my therapy groups, struggled with a history of depression and thoughts of suicide. By the time Carrie joined our group, she had been seeing an individual therapist for several years and was also stabilized on medication to treat her depression. Carrie was an active, engaged member of our group. Insightful and involved, she was consistently willing to talk about her own issues as well as lend a listening ear to her fellow group members. One day when Carrie stopped talking in group, I expressed my concerns out loud to the group. I noticed that in addition to Carrie's sudden withdrawal, she had stopped wearing her customary tank tops and shorts and had begun wearing long-sleeved shirts and long pants in the Washington, D.C. summer heat. The group gently tried to help her talk about what she was feeling, but Carrie remained withdrawn. Several weeks passed with the group continuing to lend support before Carrie revealed to everyone that she had been using a razor blade to make cuts on her legs and arms. With empathy and concern, the group encouraged Carrie to share her secret with her parents in order to get the help that she needed. If the group had not seen the changes in Carrie and asked her about them, she would not have revealed the secret that was plaguing her.

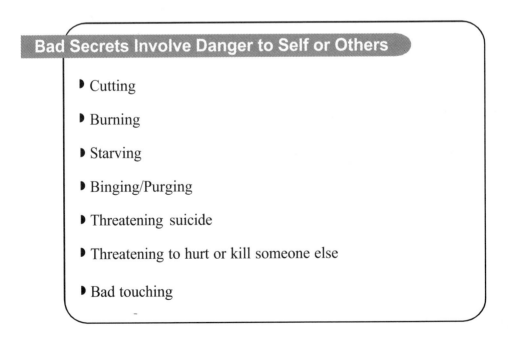

Bad Secrets Involve Danger to Self or Others

- Cutting

- Burning

- Starving

- Binging/Purging

- Threatening suicide

- Threatening to hurt or kill someone else

- Bad touching

Understanding Self-Injurious Behavior

Teenagers who self-injure engage in deliberate, repeated acts of physical harm to their own bodies. Usually the behavior is carried out in secret. A common form of self-injury is cutting. Others include slashing, scraping, burning, and biting. Even though the wounds themselves are not life-threatening, these behaviors are *always* a cry for help and should be taken seriously. Teens that injure themselves are feeling a lot of pain and are at risk for depression and anxiety. They are especially vulnerable because frequently they are detached from the feelings that drive their behavior. Initially, self-injury brings a feeling of relief and calm. The self-inflicted violence is an attempt to soothe and gain control over overwhelming feelings. The eventual consequences of self-injury, however, are feelings of helplessness and alienation.

If a child reveals to you that she's injuring herself, or if you see the signs of self-harm (slashes on arms or legs, burn marks, etc.), you have a responsibility to inform the child's parents. These kids need professional help, ideally with a therapist who specializes in self-injurious behaviors and related disorders.

Red Flags – Signs of Self-Injurious Behavior

> Long-sleeved shirts, even in warm weather

> Tiny slash marks on upper arms or legs

> Cigarette or lighter burns on skin

> Bite marks on hands or arms

> Ongoing scabbing

> Other forms of self-destructive behaviors such as reckless driving, practicing unsafe sex, eating disorders

In a group setting, kids who self-injure may have a destructive impact on the group as a whole. The attention the child receives from well-intentioned peers frequently exacerbates rather than reduces the behaviors. Occasionally, other kids in the group begin to undertake similar self-damaging behaviors as a way of fitting in and gaining attention themselves. It's best to take action as soon as you become aware of the behavior to prevent the "wildfire" effect. Ask the teen whether she wants to tell her parents herself or whether she wants you to tell them. If she volunteers to do it, follow up to make sure the parents have been informed and that they are seeking treatment for their child. If your group is aware of the behavior, reassure them that the teen is receiving the help she needs outside of group.

I've been doing staff training and consulting with summer camps for several years. I've noticed that the phenomenon of self-harm appears to be on the rise, particularly in the girls' bunks. One summer camp decided to cope with the self-injurious behavior of one of its campers internally, by offering lots of support and attention from the counselors and campers alike. Within a week, there were three more girls engaging in the same cutting behavior. As soon as the original girl was sent home to get professional help, the other campers stopped their own self-injurious behavior.

Understanding Eating Disorders

Ashley has a serious eating disorder called Bulimia Nervosa. Bulimia involves weight control through a cycle of binge eating followed by purging, either through vomiting or use of laxatives. Because a bulimic child may not lose weight, it's often easier to hide bulimia than anorexia. Kids with bulimia are at risk for muscular weakness, heart problems, electrolyte imbalance, tooth decay, and mouth ulcers. Anorexia Nervosa, another type of eating disorder, involves extreme weight loss that can lead to muscle deterioration, low blood pressure, long-term disability, and even death.

Like Ashley, many children and teenagers with eating disorders are secretive about their issues with food. Their feelings of shame are so strong that they are reluctant to talk to anyone about what they're doing. It's not uncommon for kids with eating disorders to completely deny their condition. The longer they go without treatment, however, the more entrenched the disorder becomes.

Red Flags – Eating Disorders

- Dramatic weight loss

- Frequent skipping of meals with excuses for not eating

- A distorted body image

- Excessive exercise

- Wearing baggy clothes to cover up thinness

- Making food for others but refusing to eat it

- Frequently weighing oneself

- Secretive behavior immediately after meals

- Eating large quantities of food at one time with no weight gain

- Eating mints or gum to cover up odor of vomit

- Discolored teeth

- Drinking excessive amounts of water

- Chewing food into tiny miniscule bits

If one of your group members exhibits any of these symptoms, it may be time to refer her for professional help.

It's fortunate that Nina decided to report Ashley's destructive eating behavior. Many teenagers will not take the risk of losing a friendship and will unwittingly collude with a friend by not revealing a bad secret like this one. Ms. King has a responsibility to let Ashley's parents know what has been observed about Ashley's behavior so that they can find her the help she needs.

You can respond with one of the following statements when a child reveals a bad secret to you.

Try Saying This:

"Secrets that worry you or make you sad are the ones that need to be told. I'm glad you shared this with me."

"I'm glad you chose not to carry the burden of this secret alone. You know that your friend needs help."

"Your friend may not be happy with you for telling me this. But, do know that you're doing your best to get help for your friend."

Helping Kids with Suicidal Thoughts

Hopefully you will never have to hear these dreaded words out of a child's mouth, "I want to kill myself." It's so frightening for us to think that a youngster could be so desperately unhappy as to want to end her own life. But when you work long and closely enough with children, and if you're the kind of leader that's open to hearing the private thoughts of your kids, you need to be prepared for the worst. A child may not always express suicidal thoughts verbally. Instead, leaders need to be aware of behaviors that indicate a child may be considering suicide.

Red Flags – Suicidal Thinking

- Reckless behavior such as driving while intoxicated

- Withdrawal from friends and family

- Explosive episodes of anger

- Sudden plummet in grades at school

- An obsession with death

- Talking to a friend about suicide

> ## Reminder
>
> **Establish the seriousness of the threat by asking the child directly if she has considered suicide and, if so, when and how. Broaching the subject does *not* give the child the idea to commit suicide!**

You may be thinking to yourself right now, "I hear children threaten to kill themselves all the time! They don't mean it. They are usually just seeking attention!" You may very well be right. The child could be using desperate language to communicate feelings rather than intent. But, do you really want to take the chance? What if you are wrong?

When a child threatens to kill herself under any circumstance, even if you think she's not serious, notify her parents. That way the family can make a thoughtful decision as to whether or not professional help is needed.

> ## Reminder
>
> **Teach your group members that they cannot afford to keep the secret of a friend who intends to hurt herself.**

Coping with Threats to Harm Others

If a child reveals that she or someone she knows has a plan to hurt or kill another person, *take it seriously*! You must report this to your local police. It may seem obvious, but kids who threaten violence are more likely to *be* violent. The kids in your group should be taught to tell you or another adult if they know that someone is threatening to hurt another.

Red Flags – Homicidal Thinking

▶ History of exposure to violence at home or school

▶ Carrying a weapon to feel safe from others

▶ Frequently threatens to harm or kill others

▶ Focus on "getting even" with others

▶ Substance abuse

▶ Stockpiling weapons

▶ Increasing rebellion and anger

▶ Increasing withdrawal and secrecy

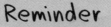

Reminder

**Immediately notify the child's
parents of your concerns.**

Secrets about Abuse

Child abuse consists of any act, or failure to act, that puts a child at risk for physical or emotional hurt.

Physical abuse – an injury resulting from physical aggression

▶ Beating

▶ Kicking, throwing, shoving, shaking

▶ Pinching or biting

- Burning with cigarettes, scalding water, or other hot objects

- Hair pulling

- Choking

Sexual abuse – any sexual act between an adult and a child

- Penetration

- Incest

- Oral sex

- Sodomy

- Fondling

- Violations of privacy

- Exposure to adult sexuality

- Commercial sexual exploitation

Emotional abuse – behavior that interferes with a child's mental health

- Verbal abuse

- Intimidation

- Belittling

- Exposure to violence against others

- Severe punishment (e.g., locking in closet)

Neglect – Failure to provide for a child's basic needs of food, shelter, and medical care

If you suspect one of your kids is being sexually or physically abused, you *must* report it to your local law enforcement agency. It's not your job to determine if, in fact, the child is telling the truth. Your job is to let the professionals do their job by making the report. Reporting is anonymous. The au-

thorities have a responsibility to investigate before taking any action to remove a child from her home.

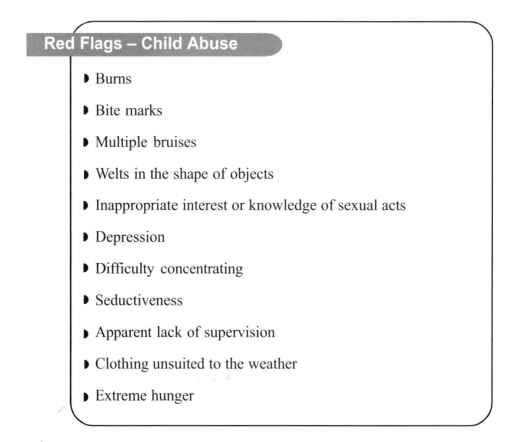

Red Flags – Child Abuse

- Burns

- Bite marks

- Multiple bruises

- Welts in the shape of objects

- Inappropriate interest or knowledge of sexual acts

- Depression

- Difficulty concentrating

- Seductiveness

- Apparent lack of supervision

- Clothing unsuited to the weather

- Extreme hunger

There are secrets that make you feel uncomfortable inside. These are the
secrets that keep you awake at night, distract you, and make you feel queasy.
Trust these feelings. They're telling you that someone is in danger and may
need help.

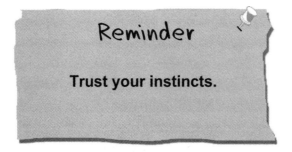

Reminder

Trust your instincts.

A Note about Gossip

Encourage your kids to treat secrets as a private matter. Gossip worsens most problems. As an adult, resist the urge to gossip yourself, particularly in front of your kids. Sharing gossip can make you feel interesting and powerful in the short term, but ultimately you feel lousy after the fact. It may make you feel like you are connecting with your kids if they share gossip with you. It can be hard to resist asking for more information or eagerly expressing your interest in the gossip. I urge you to stay clear of gossip. It creates a negative environment for a group. Continually remind yourself that you are the adult in the group, and it is up to you to create a safe, positive environment.

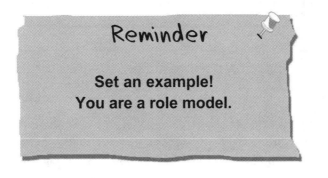

Reminder

**Set an example!
You are a role model.**

Let's Talk
Improving Communication

It drives Kim crazy when the kids in her group talk over one other. Nobody listens! The outspoken kids constantly control the group discussions, leaving no room for others to interject. The monopolizers don't seem to notice when they are losing their audience, as they continually interrupt others and charge forward with their own thoughts. The more reserved group members are left feeling frustrated, but helpless to change the chaotic group dynamic. Instead, they withdraw from group conversation by either tuning out or physically removing themselves from the discussions. Kim wants to encourage healthy conversation within the group. She knows how important it is for the children to learn good communication and listening skills while they are young.

How to Help Kids Become Good Communicators

Kids, just like adults, long to connect with others. Effective communication gets them there. Strong leaders set a powerful example of good communication for their kids. Children learn necessary communication skills by seeing and hearing the skills you model for them.

In our *Stepping Stones* program, the communication phase is one of the most vital skill sets for kids to master if they are to be able to get along with their peers. Without solid communication skills, kids are unable to relate to others successfully. A group setting is the ideal place to practice and learn these skills. It's not easy to listen and communicate in a group. There is a lot going on that makes the process challenging. As a group leader, you have a grand opportunity to help your kids develop these essential life skills.

1 Follow the do's and don'ts of communication.

Review the do's and don'ts of communication with your group. Write them down and post them in a visible place. Review them periodically and give the kids positive reinforcement when they succeed in communicating well. Ask the kids to add to the list as new do's and don'ts are observed.

Do's	Don'ts
Wait for a pause before you speak.	Don't hog the conversation.
Ask appropriate questions.	Don't change the subject too quickly.
Use a pleasant and clear tone of voice.	Don't interrupt others when they talk.
Make eye contact when speaking.	Don't finish another person's thoughts.
Hear the other person out.	Don't get caught up in too many details.
Make active-listening statements.	Don't play "I can top that!"

2 Encourage and model good eye contact.

Eye contact is one of the best ways to make another person feel acknowledged, and is the first step in the give-and-take required for a successful conversation. It is also the foundation upon which more subtle and complex communication skills are built.

In the adult world, people who don't look you straight in the eye are viewed as untrustworthy, lacking in self-confidence, or self-absorbed. In a child's world, kids view peers who don't look at them as distracted, disconnected, or disinterested. It is impossible to understand the cues others give you without first looking them in the eye and tuning in to their feelings and experiences.

Try periodically to "freeze" the discussion in your group to see which children are looking at the speaker. When you ask the speaker which children he feels are listening, notice how he inevitably names those who are looking at him. Children are drawn to those who make them feel good about themselves by looking at them and listening.

Reminder

Make sure the children are looking at you when you speak to them.

③ Practice active listening.

What do I mean by active listening? This is not just ordinary listening. Active listening lets the speaker know he is being listened to. Active listening is an extremely important component of effective communication.

It's easy to teach children to use active listening words in conversation. In Kim's group, several of the more verbal kids have trouble showing physically that they are listening, even if, in fact, they are. Kim must ask her group members to choose a couple of strategies to show others that they are listening. What works for one may not work for another. One child may want to simply nod his head in affirmation when another child speaks; another may choose to say, "Uh huh" or "Oh" or "Wow."

Ask the children in your group how they feel when their fellow group members use active listening signals. I bet they say that they feel more connected to others when they are listened to.

4 Discourage interrupting.

Let the group members know how important it is to listen patiently to one another. One of the biggest challenges of being a good conversationalist is remaining attentive. Make sure you listen to each child without interrupting and that you gently steer conversations back to the speaker when disruptions occur.

Try Saying This:

"I can't hear Jack when he is interrupted."

"I can hear Sally better when everyone is quiet."

"Julian, finish what you're saying. We are all listening."

"Each person will get a chance to speak without interruption. Let's start with Pete."

5 Emphasize the importance of listening skills to friendship.

Some of the kids in your group will be genuinely disinterested and somewhat self-absorbed, and will have no desire to listen to their peers. Naturally, you have a greater challenge with children who lack interest and empathy for other children. For these kids, it's critical to help them understand that they can't make a friend without being a friend. You must continually emphasize the feelings of others by saying things like, "How would you feel if…?" Our culture values independence and self-determination in children, but these traits can lead to a decrease in children's abilities to identify and relate to the needs of others. Independence and connection are not mutually exclusive concepts. Help your group members value the opinions and desires of others so that they can develop lasting friendships.

6 Play a game of conversation catch.

The more reserved kids in Kim's group need to do more than just listen – they have to learn ways to keep the conversation moving forward. Good conversation requires give-and-take – just like a game of catch. The speaker throws the ball to the listener. The listener catches the ball by using active listening words. The listener then throws it back by asking a question that expresses interest, or by making a statement that shows understanding. Then the speaker returns the ball by continuing the conversation on the same subject. In order to have a satisfying game of catch, or a satisfying conversation, the ball needs to go back and forth more than a couple of times before the game stops.

Some children don't know how to keep things going. They genuinely cannot think of what to say next. You'll find it helpful to play the "What Comes Next?" game with these kids to give them ideas about how to keep conversation alive.

"What Comes Next?" Game

This game will help your group deepen their conversations. If your kids have some down time, suggest they play this game with you.

One group member brings up a topic of conversation.

The group shouts "What comes next?"

Another group member must then think of a comment or question to ask that relates to the topic and will keep the conversation going.

The group shouts "What comes next?" after each response.

This continues like a game of catch until the topic of conversation has been exhausted.

Count how many times a comment or question can be made before a conversation is finished. Encourage the group to exceed their previous score in the next conversation.

"What Comes Next?" Example

Joy: "I saw the best movie the other day!"

Group: "What comes next?"

Will: "Really? Which one did you see?"

Group: "What comes next?"

Joy: "'Mean Girls'! I could totally relate to it!"

Group: "What comes next?"

Haley: "I saw that movie. I really liked it too."

Group: "What comes next?"

Joy: "My favorite part was the end. What was yours?"

Group: "What comes next?"

Haley: "I liked when Cady gave Regina that stuff that made her skin break out."

Group: "What comes next?"

Liza: "Yeah! That was so gross!"

Group: "What comes next?"

7 Verify the message.

Sometimes communication is misinterpreted, which can lead to trouble if there's no clarification. As the listener, model for the kids that it's okay to ask, "What do you mean?" if you don't understand, or are offended by something someone is saying. Asking for more information ensures that the message and its intent are clear.

Try Saying This:

"Am I getting this right….?"

"What do you mean when you say….?"

"I don't understand. Can you clarify?"

"So, what I'm hearing you say is…."

⑧ Clarify your expectations.

To avoid frustration or disappointment, make sure that you are as clear and concrete as possible in your requests of the group. Be specific and define exactly what you want.

Try Saying This:

"I will know when you are finished when all of the toys are off the floor, dirty clothes are in the hamper, and the beds are made."

"During warm-ups, I expect you to clap twice every time a teammate makes a lay-up and to clap once every time the shot doesn't go in."

"Before you pass the ball, you must yell out the person's name that you're passing to."

⑨ Avoid questions or statements that shut down communication.

There are certain statements and questions that adults frequently ask kids that irritate them. It's best to avoid those, if possible.

"How does that make you feel?" (Makes you sound too much like a therapist.)

"I know how you feel." (You probably don't.)

"Why did you do that?" (They usually don't know the answer, so why ask?)

"You know what I mean?" (Makes you sound unsure of yourself.)

"Yes, but…" (This indicates that you are not listening.)

"Did you have a good time?" (Dead-end question)

10 Tune in to nonverbal communication.

Without uttering a single word, our bodies and facial expressions communicate a lot about how we feel. Be aware of your own body language, tone of voice, and facial expressions at all times because whether you like it or not, they tell your whole story. Your nonverbal communication is heard loud and clear by your kids.

When Kim is frustrated with her group's frenzied communication, she typically has a frown on her face, her arms are crossed, and her body is tense. There is no doubt about what she's feeling inside, and the kids pick up on it. On the other hand, if Kim nods her head, smiles, and her body is relaxed, she is communicating nonverbally, "I am listening to you. I am with you."

Some children are better at reading nonverbal cues than others. Some kids can tell that you have had a bad day just by looking at you. Other kids do not pick up on nonverbal communication at all, or they interpret it inaccurately. For these kids, you must interpret body language and facial expressions for them.

"Did you notice that when Felix is getting frustrated, his face turns red?"

"I know something is bugging you because I see you're sitting here in the corner with your head down and a frown on your face."

"I'm going to stop asking Mark questions because I can see that I'm irritating him. I notice the way his hands are clenched and he's answering me through clenched teeth."

11 Play communication games.

Practicing good communication skills is like practicing a musical instrument or a sport. Everyone needs to practice, but different levels of natural talent will require different amounts of effort. For some kids, the need for consistent rehearsal is essential to give them the confidence they need to communicate effectively. Try the following games to help your kids beef up their conversation skills. We use many of these in our *Stepping Stones* social skills training groups. The continuous practice of these communication skills helps the kids transfer learned social skills from our group to their home and school environments. The *Stepping Stones* group members love playing these games, and they even play them at home with their parents!

The Story Game

Tell a story together as a group, taking turns. You begin. When you stop, it's a child's turn to continue the story. It's important that group members wait their turn before speaking, and that each part of the story connects in some way to the previous piece of the story that was just told.

The Conversation Game

You will need a small container and some pennies or poker chips for this game. The goal of the game is for the group to earn more than 25 chips/pennies. A group member begins a conversation. Using the chips/pennies as rewards, place two chips/pennies in the container for every relevant question that is asked after the opening statement. Place one chip/penny into the container for every statement made that is relevant. A chip/penny is removed from the container each time someone doesn't wait for a pause to speak, or when someone abruptly changes the subject.

The TV Talk Show Host Game

All the kids in the group interview one another as if they were on a TV talk show. If you can videotape the talk show game so the kids can see it later, that's even better. The host of the talk show has three goals:

1. Help make your guest feel more comfortable by using active-listening techniques.

2. Ask questions of your guest that show interest.

3. Share information about yourself that relates to your guest's topic.

The guest has three goals:

1. Answer the host's questions politely and appropriately.

2. Stay focused on the topic.

3. Use active-listening skills.

Ask the kids to swap roles so they can experience both sides during the game.

Do What I Say *and* What I Do Game

Divide the group into pairs. One person draws a picture that their partner cannot see. The artist's goal is to have his partner draw exactly the same picture. To accomplish this, the artist must give clear, accurate verbal directions to lead the partner to the finished product.

Effective communication is critical to a successful group. Through your communication as the leader, both verbal and nonverbal, you not only help foster connections within your group, you'll also help the kids learn how to develop give-and-take relationships outside of the group.

Reminder

Great leaders are great communicators!

Mismatched Co-leaders
Learning to Work in Tandem

Mark and Dan are Little League coaches. Mark's twelve-year-old son is on the team. As the head coach, Mark is excited to have the opportunity to work with Dan. He knows from a technical standpoint, it doesn't get much better than Dan. Dan played minor league baseball when he was young and knows the game inside and out. By contrast, Mark played baseball only in high school. His goal for coaching is, above all else, to have fun. He wants to take advantage of the quality time to bond with his son. Mark is confident that Dan will fill in any gap in experience that he lacks.

(Fast forward one month.)

It has become clear that Mark and Dan's coaching styles are not as complementary as Mark presumed they'd be. Mark's focus on teamwork and relationship building drives Dan crazy. Dan's main objective is to teach the kids the necessary skills to win games. Because Mark is more laid back, Dan feels it's up to him to whip the team into shape. He takes on the dominant coaching position because he feels Mark's passivity will lead the team to failure. His authoritarian approach takes the form of screaming at players throughout the games, fighting with other coaches on the field, and yelling at umpires when the calls are not to his liking. His aggressive conduct with *the umpires is severe enough to get him kicked out of several games. The players are afraid of him. The parents are upset with his treatment of the team, and they're looking to Mark to fix the situation. They are furious with Mark for allowing Dan's destructive behavior to continue.*

By mid-season, the parents, the players, and the coaches are miserable, but they are at a loss as to what to do to rectify a very tense, unhappy situation.

In an ideal world, co-leaders would demonstrate the following principles:

Leadership Principles

▶ Teach children skills to enhance their abilities.

▶ Model appropriate behavior at all times.

▶ Encourage teamwork and good sportsmanship in the group.

▶ Treat each child equally; do not show favoritism or bias toward any one child.

▶ Be respectful of others.

▶ Communicate openly and effectively with co-leaders.

▶ Create an atmosphere to have fun!

Unfortunately, these goals are rarely met. Many parent coaches fall into the trap of focusing too much attention on their own child. Sometimes the attention is overly positive; frequently coaches are harder on their own child than they are on the rest of the team (refer to chapter N – Nepotism/Fighting Favoritism). Sometimes coaches get involved in coaching for self-serving reasons, putting the needs of the team second to their own agenda.

In addition, co-leaders commonly struggle to effectively communicate with each other. As in the case of Mark and Dan, their goals and leadership styles clash, leaving them and their team members in a state of unrest. When group leaders are not on the same page, the kids are the ones who suffer most.

Positive Co-leadership

1 **Discuss your goals and objectives up front.**

Don't assume that you and your co-leader share the same goals. Work them out before the group starts, and communicate them out loud to each other. Better yet, write them down. Your productivity and accountability as leaders automatically rise when you not only write the goals down, but print and distribute them to the kids and their parents. The wonderful thing about well-publicized goals and objectives is that you can use them to evaluate yourselves as co-leaders. If you have trouble following your own plan, then you can refer back to the standards in your shared agreement to help you get back on course.

Sample List of Goals

- Model good sportsmanship and teamwork for our players at all times.

- Treat our players and all others with respect and fairness.

- Create a place for our kids to have fun.

- Teach and enhance skills in our players in a productive way.

- Communicate appropriately and openly with our kids and each other.

- Do our best to meet the needs and expectations of the group.

② Discuss your strengths and weaknesses at the onset.

There is no getting around the fact that everyone has strengths and weaknesses. The key is to be self-aware and communicative with your co-leader about your strengths and weaknesses. Create a worksheet with two columns, one for strengths and one for weaknesses, and have co-leaders fill out both sides of the paper with an equal number of strengths and weaknesses (see Dan and Mark's lists below). You will notice that many co-leaders have no trouble listing weaknesses, but find it difficult to list strengths. Other leaders are the opposite and can't see their weaknesses. Help each other fill out the worksheet. Be careful not to judge your co-leader's responses. Once you have both named your strong and weak points, then you can develop a plan for accentuating the positives in both of you and working around the weaknesses.

Imagine if Dan and Mark had gone through this process together.

Dan's Leadership Strengths	Dan's Leadership Weaknesses
▶ I know the game of baseball well.	▶ I can be hotheaded.
▶ I can develop strong players through skill building.	▶ I can be hard on the kids.
▶ I can make this team a winning team.	▶ I don't like to lose, and I show it.

Mark's Leadership Strengths	Mark's Leadership Weaknesses
▶ I am an excellent team builder. ▶ I make the game fun for the kids. ▶ I consistently model good sportsmanship.	▶ I avoid conflict. ▶ When stressed, I become passive. Parents and players may consider this a weakness. ▶ My focus on fun may be perceived as not taking my job seriously enough.

Reminder

Weaknesses are a lightning rod for negative attention; strengths are the key to achieving positive results.

Define leadership roles up front.

Once you have agreed upon goals and objectives and you have communicated openly about your strengths and weaknesses, now you are ready to develop a leadership plan. Reinforce positive behaviors by adopting roles that play to both of your strengths.

Read Mark and Dan's list above. Mark, as head coach, could have capitalized on Dan's skill-building abilities by delineating an active role for him during practices where he could easily do what he does best – teach the game of baseball. Looking openly at Dan's weaknesses, however, while taking advantage of Mark's strengths, clearly indicates a more active role for Mark during the games, where the overall team goal is sportsmanship and team building.

You and your co-leader are going to be much happier and work much harder if you work on things you're each interested in and feel strongly about. This may mean that the division of responsibilities with your co-leader is different than you imagined. Be flexible and willing to change roles over time if they're not working.

In a social skills group I recently observed, the two therapists leading the group had decided that one of them would play the role of the "behavioral enforcer" — putting stars on the blackboard when she saw positive behavior. She was also the one who enforced consequences when the rules were not followed. The other therapist was in charge of helping the kids practice the skills they were learning. It didn't take long for the therapists to realize that their roles needed to be reversed. The "behavioral enforcer" was much more comfortable working with the group process and the interaction between the kids. The other therapist managed the overall group behavior with ease and confidence. Embracing flexibility to change their roles helped the therapists make the group run more smoothly and effectively.

4 Set up a regular schedule for an open, ongoing dialogue.

It's important to meet regularly with your co-leader. Set an agreed upon meeting time. It doesn't matter what day or what time, as long as it's regular and predictable.

It is obviously going to be easier to communicate with a co-leader who is similar to you. In a simpatico co-leadership, you are tuned into each other's needs and can clearly communicate ideas without fear of misunderstanding. Fostering positive communication with a co-leader you don't relate well to is trickier. Make it a priority to monitor the quality of your communication skills. (Practice the skills you learned in the "Let's Talk" chapter.)

Communication Boosters

▶ Give your co-leader your full attention when he speaks.

▶ Try to maintain a good balance between talking and listening.

▶ Ask open-ended questions that encourage discussion.

▶ Restate thoughts and feelings to be sure you understand them correctly.

▶ Watch your co-leader's body language and facial expression to deepen your understanding of him.

▶ React positively to your co-leader's ideas.

▶ Stay clear of giving advice unless asked directly for it.

▶ When you disagree, try to see it from the other person's perspective.

▶ Give feedback in a constructive manner.

5 Begin the habit of soliciting input from each other.

If you are the main leader, it is especially important for you to solicit the help of your subordinates. People need to know that their opinions are valued. By asking directly for feedback and ideas, you are demonstrating your respect for your co-leader. Make a point of recognizing and acknowledging their perspective.

Try Saying This:

"What do you think we should do?"

"How would you handle this situation?"

"I need your help figuring out this problem."

6 Debrief consistently with and without the children present.

Leaders constantly find opportunities to review the group's performance. After a game, coaches meet with their players to highlight the positive plays in the game as well as the ways the team can improve. At the end of the school day, teachers review with their students what was learned and talk about ways to improve performance and behavior in the future. Theatre directors give notes to their actors after each rehearsal to continue to fine-tune the performance process.

Co-leaders also need time alone to debrief. Working with kids in groups can be tiring, stressful, and challenging. Take a few minutes to talk through things after a particularly difficult group meeting. This is a terrific time to praise your co-leader's actions in the group. Allow your co-leader to vent frustrations while you listen attentively. Provide support and encouragement, as well as constructive feedback to each other. Constantly reevaluate and highlight what is working in your co-leadership, as well as what isn't. Be honest with yourself and your co-leader and commit to finding solutions to challenges as they arise.

Constructive Feedback

▶ Constructive feedback is given respectfully and calmly.

▶ Constructive feedback is a two-way street. You have to be as good at receiving it as giving it.

▶ Constructive feedback emphasizes changing behavior, not character.

▶ Constructive feedback is expressed empathetically.

(7) Backup your co-leader in times of frustration.

No doubt, at some point during the life of your group, the kids are going to push your buttons, and you're going to feel frustrated, overwhelmed, or stressed. Be prepared for that reality by arranging to step in for each other when your frustration is getting in the way of effectively managing the group. What pushes one leader's buttons may not push the other's. Let the calmer of the two leaders take over when tempers are flaring. Chances are it's only a matter of time before your roles will be reversed.

This technique is frequently used by parents with their own children. When Mom is losing her temper with one of the kids, Dad moves in to take over, allowing Mom a much needed cooling-off period. This method is just as effective when working with kids in groups. I recall a moment in a teen group I was co-leading when I was taken off guard because a teenager said something provocative to me. I was so surprised that I was tongue tied for a few seconds. Luckily, as I was trying to process what I was going to say, my co-leader immediately jumped in. She didn't take the bait and confront the teen directly (which was my impulse), but rather, gently asked the rest of the group to comment on the interaction.

8 Communicate a united front.

Another principle borrowed from Parenting 101 is having co-leaders present a united front. Just as parents should be careful to send consistent messages to their children, you and your co-leader must agree on rules and expectations for the group *before* engaging with the kids. If one leader is communicating one thing while the other is saying something else, the kids become confused and anxious. Keep your disagreements in front of the children to a minimum. If you have differences, work them out privately and then present clear information to the kids.

In Dan and Mark's case, Mark was strongly opposed to Dan's behavior with the kids, and he wisely chose not to share his feelings in front of the parents and players. Confronting Dan during a game would surely have resulted in an ugly scene. Unfortunately, Mark didn't raise his issues with Dan in their personal meetings either. Thus, the destructive behavior continued unchecked.

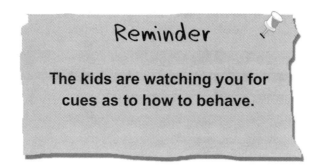

Reminder

The kids are watching you for cues as to how to behave.

9 Let volatile situations calm down before addressing them.

Make an agreement with your co-leader to discuss difficult issues, but not during emotionally heated times. When under emotional stress, you are more likely to strike a defensive tone and less willing to listen or negotiate. The discussion will not be productive. Table it until emotions calm down.

Take time-outs to check in with your co-leader.

Sometimes you need to stop the group action in the moment to check in with your co-leader. Ask the group to freeze while you figure out your next step with your co-leader. You don't have to wait until the end of the activity to check in with your co-leader when either, or both, of you are unclear about how best to proceed in certain situations.

Use humor whenever possible.

Laughter feels good. Humor cushions us against life's inevitable ups and downs. Whenever you are feeling too serious or stressed, look at yourself through the lens of humor and watch how quickly you relax. Being able to laugh at yourself and not take things too seriously makes you a much more approachable leader. When there is a lot of tension in the group, humor can be a great way to diffuse it and allow everyone to move on from a difficult moment.

However, make sure that your humor is timely and appropriate. Nobody wants to be on the receiving end of a bad joke. Be careful about your use of sarcasm with children. Many kids don't understand sarcasm, and adults frequently use it to cover up underlying anger. If you are indeed angry, figure out how to effectively communicate it rather than resorting to sarcasm. (See the chapter on "Understanding Your Emotions" for anger management techniques.)

A positive relationship with your co-leader makes a very powerful impact on your group members. Kids model their behavior on the way that you and your co-leader work together, resolve conflicts, and adapt to your distinct roles. Putting some energy and time into the co-leader relationship up front is worthwhile. The fruits of your labor will bear out in the balance and harmony in your group.

Nepotism
Fighting Favoritism

Eileen believes that she treats all of her students equally. She considers herself scrupulously fair and gives no one student any more special attention than any other student. A strict teacher, Eileen enforces a structured classroom setting with consistent disciplinary methods. She clearly communicates her expectations for assignments and grading criteria in class. Eileen has noticed that each year, several of her students are highly motivated and easy to inspire. Others float through the class with little interest or enthusiasm. Eileen is not disappointed or frustrated with this predictable pattern – she sees it as the reality of teaching a group of middle-school students.

Eileen is shocked to learn that this year, many of the boys in her class (and their parents) are accusing her of playing favorites. They say that she gives extra attention to the girls, and tends to focus more on the boys' negative behavior in class rather than their positive contributions. In addition, the boys feel that she chooses literature for the class that is female dominated. The boys can't relate because the books mostly contain strong female characters rather than strong male ones. Eileen is not sure how seriously to take these complaints. Part of her believes that these boys are looking for excuses to misbehave in her class. Another part of her, however, asks herself the question, "Am I giving the girls in my class preferential treatment?"

It is common to feel yourself drawn to certain kids more than others. You are human, after all! There are always children who remind you fondly of yourself as a child, or of a beloved nephew or niece. Similarly, you may have negative reactions to certain kids who push your buttons. For unknown reasons, you may feel more disconnected from them and even repelled by them. The following are steps you can take to keep favoritism at a minimum:

① Acknowledge your preferences.

You'll notice patterns in your work with children. You may consistently feel drawn to kids with particular personality and character traits. For instance, you may feel closer to children who make you laugh and share your sense of humor. If you are athletic, you may feel most connected with kids who are also interested in watching and playing sports. Perhaps you're the type of leader who is always attracted to the child with a difficult home life. This child pulls on your heart strings and makes you feel needed as a caretaker and a mentor. It doesn't matter what the reason is for your subjective feelings about the kids in your group. What is important is that you are aware of these feelings.

> ## Reminder
>
> **It is only through awareness that you can maintain objectivity as a leader.**

Although many adult leaders, including Eileen, believe that they are above favoritism, few actually are. Gender frequently is a factor in favoritism. Girls may be favored because they behave better in group situations. Eileen may see her girls as more active participants in classroom discussions than the boys. It's very possible that while she encourages the girls, she unwittingly discourages the boys. Without recognizing her tendency to favor girls, Eileen may be inadvertently disenfranchising the boys in her classroom.

② Never assume.

Even though you have every intention of treating your kids fairly, you may make subtle assumptions about individual kids. When this happens, you end up treating the children differently. For instance, you have to be very careful about making cultural assumptions. To assume that all African-American children learn in the same way, or that all Latino kids have identical backgrounds, is to set the stage for biased treatment. You can't base your understanding of an individual child on race or any other single dimension. Take the time to get to know each child on a one-to-one basis.

③ Look for the strengths in each child.

In a perfect universe, you would like all of the kids in your group equally. But this is not a perfect universe. Some children are going to be harder for you to like than others. And it is with these kids that you will have a more difficult time finding and reinforcing their strengths. Don't give up. If you look hard enough, you can always find a child's positive attributes. The more you learn about a child, the more likely it is that you will find something you like about him. The following are a list of questions you can ask yourself to help you understand and appreciate what is unique about each kid.

Strength-Finding Questions

"What about this particular child is unique and special?"

"What excites this child?"

"How can I make this child laugh?"

"What interests this child?"

"What does this child contribute to the group?"

Now that you know more about this child, you can pay closer attention to his strengths and look for opportunities to foster an individual connection with him. This levels the playing field and lessens the likelihood of favoritism.

4 Positively reframe negative traits.

The qualities that make it hard for you to favor a child can easily be reframed in a positive light. This is a great way to make *all* of your children into your favorites!

Try Saying This to Yourself:	Rather Than This:
"This child is passionate in his beliefs."	"This child is opinionated."
"This child is assertive and able to get his needs met."	"This child is demanding."
"This child is full of energy."	"This child is hyper."
"This child is spontaneous."	"This child is impulsive."
"This child is insecure."	"This child is snobbish and uninvolved."

5 Divide your attention evenly.

Distributing your interest equally among a group of kids is much easier said than done. And children are extremely sensitive to feeling left out, especially by adults. Your natural inclination may be to give more floor time to children who are verbally outgoing. And then there are the "squeaky wheels" who you have to constantly reprimand, correct, and refocus when they misbehave. These kids end up receiving a disproportionate amount of your attention, even though it's negative. Kids are unable to differentiate between negative and positive attention – what they see is that while you're occupied with one child, you are not available to another. Figure out a way to track your attention time with each member of your group.

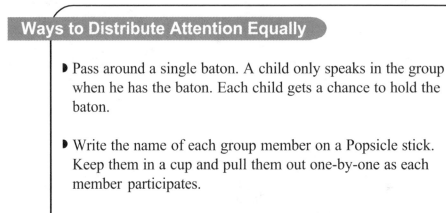

Ways to Distribute Attention Equally

▶ Pass around a single baton. A child only speaks in the group when he has the baton. Each child gets a chance to hold the baton.

▶ Write the name of each group member on a Popsicle stick. Keep them in a cup and pull them out one-by-one as each member participates.

▶ Sit in a circle. Going around the circle, take turns speaking.

▶ Ask often, "Who haven't we heard from recently?"

▶ Frequently say aloud how each group member uniquely contributes to the group.

▶ Use nonverbal communication frequently, e.g., a pat on the back, a nod or a smile directed at a particular group member.

6 Be open to being observed.

In Eileen's case, she questions the veracity of the boys' assertions, wondering if they're merely seeking excuses for bad behavior. Unaware of any feelings of favoritism, Eileen needs an objective reality check. She might consider enlisting the aid of a neutral observer. A trusted colleague can have useful insights to share. Ask a coworker to sit in on one of your groups and observe your interactions with the kids. Be open to their honest feedback.

7 Be clear about your boundaries.

There is a line between recognizing and supporting a child's abilities and crossing boundaries. As a leader, you will encounter kids who see you as a lifesaver. Not all children have caring parents and other adults in their lives who believe in them. You play a vital role in these kids' lives. So, what's wrong with inviting a child who loves the theatre to a performance? Or taking a kid to lunch to discuss his future? Although these actions come from a place of good intentions, you have to make sure that you offer the same support and guidance to all of your kids. Ask yourself if the unique benefits you present to one child are offered to all of your kids equally.

8 Pair up the kids.

You know the expression, "Opposites attract." This applies to children's relationships too. Human beings can bring out the best (and the worst) in each other. Notice how one child's strengths balances another child's weaknesses (and vice versa). If you're struggling to connect with one of your kids, enlist another child to do it for you. If possible, pair up children who complement each other. For instance, if one of your group members is outspoken and gregarious, team him up with a child who is reserved and thoughtful to complete an assignment or project together. Then, you can observe aloud how well the pair collaborates, showing favoritism to neither and both at the same time.

9 Help the kids see themselves as a group, not as individual competitors.

You can avoid favoritism completely when you focus on the group as a whole, rather than on any individual members. When you work together as a team, you are less likely to focus attention on one child and your group will become stronger and more cohesive.

Try Saying This:

"You really know how to work together to meet our goal!"

"When you put your heads together, there is no stopping you!"

"Wow! Eight heads are definitely better than one! How did you guys come up with that solution?"

"All of you add so much to this group. Look how well we do when we all work as a team!"

It's very important to be sensitive and caring to all of your group members. Each child has unique personality traits and talents for you to appreciate. You will not feel nor relate to each child in the same way – it's unrealistic to expect otherwise. However, as a leader, it's essential that you keep a close watch over potential favoritism. You may not have control over your feelings, but you certainly want to be in charge of your actions while the kids are in your care.

Outside the Box
Supporting Kids from Nontraditional Families

"Why can't my family be normal?" fourteen-year-old Tina asks the group. "None of my friends have two Moms! I hate it!" Tina belongs to a support group for teens at a local community center. "Wait a minute. 'Normal?' Hmm. I'm not sure I know what a normal family is. Can someone please help me out here?" Cherie has led this group for several years. She provides a safe place where kids can air their feelings and get some needed help with their issues at home and at school. "Let me help you with this, Cherie," Tina explains sarcastically. "Family equals a couple — one male, one female. Dad works. Mom stays home to take care of the kids. That's it." "Tina, nobody I know has a family like that. Maybe on television, but definitely not in my world," Trey exclaims. "Me neither," chimes in Renee. "I'm hearing several group members say that the classic, traditional family doesn't exist anymore. Then why does Tina still feel she's not normal? Do any of you ever feel the pressure Tina feels to live in what she calls a 'normal' family?" asks Cherie. Everyone in the group nods. Trey says, "Oh, totally. You can't escape it. I live with my mom and have never even met my dad. I get asked all the time, 'Where's your dad? Why didn't you bring your dad? How come your dad never comes to any of your games?' I get so sick of explaining myself to people."

Families come in many different sizes, shapes, and colors. The "Ozzie and Harriet" world of the 1950's is nearly gone. The traditional nuclear family is no longer the only way we think of family. Nowadays, families are defined by how the family members take care of each other, rather than by the way the families are structured. Even though the nature of the American family has changed dramatically over the last fifty years, the children in a nontraditional family continue to face biases in our society. As a group leader, you have an opportunity to help these kids address the social challenges they may face.

The Many Shapes of the American Family

Let's take a look at the variety of packages families come in:

The "Classic" Married Nuclear Family

Both adults are biological parents of the children. The man works outside the home. The woman works in the home taking care of the children.

Same as above, except that the woman works outside the home. The man stays home.

Same as above, except that both the man and the woman work outside the home.

The Adoptive Married Nuclear Family

The adults are not the biological parents of the children.

The Single-Parent Family

One parent lives at home

with, and has primary custody of, the children. In this country, most single parents are women.

The Blended Family

Created by either divorce, or widowhood and remarriage, the blended family may have unrelated children living in the same household. An adult without children marrying into a family with children is also considered a blended family. The blended family union may also produce half-siblings.

The Cohabitating Family

The adults in this household are living together but are not married.

The Family with Lesbian or Gay Parents

Sometimes the adults bring children from a previous heterosexual union into the family; other times, the children are adopted or conceived through artificial insemination.

The Grandparent-led or Adult Sibling-led Family

The adult(s) in this household are grandparents or siblings who take care of the children after the parents have died or are otherwise unable to care for them.

The Extended Family

Several generations of families live in the same home and share in the parental responsibilities for the children.

The Community Family

This family is comprised of a group of adults and children who live together and share the responsibilities of raising the children. Some adults may act as primary caretakers while others function in the role of provider.

The Foster or Group Home Family

Children are taken care of by a substitute family or organization. In many cases, these are short-term arrangements until the children can be returned to their biological parents or an adoptive family is found.

The Long Distance Family

The parents may not live together because they work in different states (even countries) or they live elsewhere, except on weekends. One parent lives in the primary residence while the other visits or helps raise the children from a distance.

Although there are many different types of families, children in other than the conventional family system may feel embarrassed by their unique family constitution. In addition, some of the kids in your group who live in a traditional nuclear family may not understand the circumstances of other kids' situations. This lack of understanding may lead to insensitivity and judgment. As a group leader, you have a duty to create an environment where diversity is embraced and discussed frankly.

Here are some ways to foster openness and understanding:

1 Take stock of your own attitudes and judgments.

The kids in your group can sense any bias that you may have – children are quite amazing this way. They have the tendency to act out their leaders' feelings. Before you become a group leader make sure that you understand and let go of your own prejudices regarding what constitutes a "real family." If you don't, you run the risk of making your group intolerant and unsafe.

Know your limitations. If you are uncomfortable with a topic, stay in the background. Sometimes a little space and thought is all you need to respond appropriately to an uncomfortable situation. If, on the other hand, you are at a loss for how to deal with a nontraditional family situation, ask for guidance from a friend, a colleague, or a co-leader.

2 Recognize societal barriers.

To some extent, society may still pass negative judgment on nontraditional families. But, many of these families are becoming quite common now. As nontraditional families become the norm, society will, over time, become more tolerant and prejudice should diminish.

The family constellation that continues to be criticized in our society is that with two same-sex parents. As a result, the kids of these unions may be even more reluctant to disclose personal family information than kids of other nontraditional families. These kids need as much support from you as possible. Your comfort level (or lack thereof) sets the stage for whether it is safe for these kids to share personal information with their peers. When you communicate openness, your group members will pick up on it and follow suit. Likewise, if your feelings are negative, the group will express this too. Once you understand your own feelings, you can establish the neutral, accepting atmosphere that all leaders aspire to for their groups.

In the example at the beginning of this chapter, Cherie does a nice job of establishing an open, non-judgmental atmosphere where the teens are able to share and discuss their feelings about their families. She communicates empathy and understanding, which allows the group members to question each other in a safe and gentle manner. If you notice, Cherie also encourages the kids to help each other rather than be dependent only on her, as the leader, for guidance.

3 **Be as discrete as a child needs you to be.**

Some children in nontraditional families are completely comfortable sharing information about their family situation. They talk openly about it and are very matter-of-fact in their demeanor. These are the kids who will say, "Hey, I'm at my dad's house this weekend. Do you want to hang out with me there?" or "I'm not sure which of my moms is coming to the game today." It's very important that you go with the flow of the child in this regard. If he's open, he's telling you that his family structure is no big deal for him. No big deal for him, no big deal for you or the group.

On the other hand, a child may not want to get into explaining his family to others. If a child discloses personal information about his background to you in private, he may not want his personal matters to be common knowledge in the group. If the child is giving you that message, check it out with him.

"Juan, I notice you are telling me about your family in private. Is this because you want to keep your family a private matter?"

"I'd like to respect your privacy. If a group member asks me questions, what would be the best way for me to handle it?"

Let the kids themselves take the lead on what is shared in the group. Confidentiality should always be maintained. Many kids who are allowed to control what their peers know about their families eventually open up about their situation. When children become more comfortable with their own circumstances, their peers usually relax as well.

This can be tricky. Kids are curious beings, and they may ask questions. For instance, if two dads take turns picking up their son every day from practice, team members may ask you why Juan calls two different guys "Dad." Unless you have cleared it with Juan ahead of time, this is not your information to share. You must refer the question back to Juan to answer.

Anil: "Hey, coach, how come Juan calls two different guys 'Dad'?"

Coach: "You know, Anil. That's seems like a good question to ask Juan."

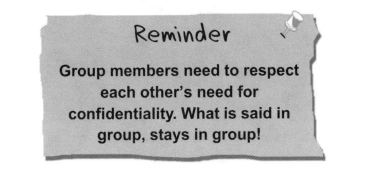

4 Accept that kids ask the darndest things.

In most cases, when kids ask questions that are insensitive and even hurtful, they are not purposely being unkind. Instead, kids frequently are unaware of the impact their questions have on others. From your point of view as a group leader, it doesn't matter whether a child's motive in asking a question is mean-spirited or innocent. It's usually best for you to respond *as if* the question is innocent. When you assume a child's question or comment is innocently motivated, you are better able to maintain neutrality and handle the situation sensitively and appropriately.

Be prepared for anything. The following questions are just a sample of what you may hear from your kids:

(Regarding adoptive families) "So, where is your 'real' mom and why did she give you away?"

(Regarding blended families) "I don't get it. Why do you live in two houses?"

(Regarding grandparent-led families) "Your mom is old." Or "Why does your grandmother always come to these things? Where's your mom?"

(Regarding commuter families) "Your parents are divorced. That's why they live in different states. Why don't you just admit it?"

(Regarding foster or group home families) "So you don't have a family? What did you do to get sent away?"

(Regarding community families) "Two dads and three moms live in your house? Do they all sleep in the same bed?"

Stay tuned in to the group's dynamics and interactions. Notice how the kids react to each other. What body language and facial expressions are you observing? How you manage a situation will vary depending on the kids' comfort level. If, when asked a question, a child answers casually and non-defensively, don't get involved. The child obviously doesn't need you to intervene.

There are going to be times, however, when you notice that a personal question makes a child uncomfortable. When you see these signs, or any other signals that the child may feel uncomfortable, consider stepping in to help, but use your best judgment about when it's appropriate.

Don't make things worse or embarrass a child by interfering when it isn't necessary. Use the following signs to help judge if a kid needs you to intervene.

Signs that a Kid Is Feeling Awkward or Uneasy

▶ The child's face blushes

▶ The child's body squirms

▶ The child answers defensively

▶ The child stutters and doesn't answer

▶ The child makes a joke

Try Saying This:

"That question is a private one, Sharon. Why don't you ask Emma after the group?"

"Can I help you out with this question, Casey?"

"There is an appropriate time and place to ask personal questions. This isn't one of them."

"Ali's body language and facial expression are telling me that he doesn't want to answer this question right now. Let's move on."

"Jacob, I'm not sure that you heard how what you just said sounded. How do you think you'd feel if someone asked you the same question about your family?"

"It doesn't look like Jesse wants to go into that right now."

5 Welcome family diversity.

Keep the lines of communication open in your group. If you notice kids showing signs of intolerance, call them on their negative behavior immediately. Let these kids know that your group welcomes diversity. Remind the group that you will not stand for prejudice or discrimination of any kind in your group.

Families are best defined as a group of people who take care of each other. As an adult leader, you will work with kids from a variety of backgrounds and family structures. Children, like adults, often make assumptions, even when they know little about a subject. These assumptions may be challenging for children in nontraditional families to reckon with. You have the opportunity to help broaden the experience of your kids by maintaining an atmosphere of openness and acceptance in your group.

Try Saying This:

"None of our families is the same. Differences make the world a whole lot more interesting."

"You just called Kim's family weird. Just because her family is different than yours doesn't make it weird."

"I think that there is some misunderstanding here about Zoe's family. Zoe, the group wants to get to know you better. Can you tell us in your own words a little about your family?"

"Wait a minute. Timothy just told us a story about a friend from a 'broken home.' Just because a child lives in two houses doesn't mean the family is broken and needs to be fixed."

Parents Are People Too
Turning Parents into Allies

Sports Day Camp is a new experience for eight-year-old Kevin. As excited as he is about getting to play sports all day long, Kevin has never been in a camp setting before. He is used to the consistent structure of elementary school and team sports. Camp is so much looser. For him, it's like being out on the playground at recess for hours on end! The counselors are having trouble with Kevin's behavior. He can't seem to control himself with the other campers. While the other kids are able to settle down and focus when asked, Kevin gets wound up and then becomes uncontrollable. He doesn't respond to the counselors' gentle reprimands and redirections. One day, during some rough housing, Kevin pushes another child down to the ground. After camp each day, Kevin's dad asks the counselors, "How did Kevin do today? Did he have a good day at camp?" Thus far, the counselors have said that he is doing just fine. After today's incident, the counselors are thinking that they need to talk to Kevin's dad about his son's behavior.

Parents play an integral role in your group's experience. Because parents are experts on their own child, they are great resources for you in working successfully with your kids. Parents are able to reinforce group concepts, skills, and lessons at home. When they are included in the group process, they can be a leader's greatest ally. Unfortunately, parents sometimes cause group leaders great stress. I can't tell you how often I ask group leaders, "What's the hardest part of leading a kids' group?" and they answer, "The parents!"

Leaders complain that parents don't want to hear "bad news" about their child, and that can impede their child's success in the group. Although some leaders successfully engage parents as allies, many do not know how to talk to parents in a constructive, positive way about their child's behavior. When a parent himself behaves badly, leaders have even more difficulty communicating effectively. For instance, when a parent yells directions from the sidelines while the team coach is trying to do his job, the child becomes confused, and the coach becomes frustrated. Many coaches would not know how to approach a parent in this type of situation without fear of offending the parent and causing an angry scene.

Similarly, the counselors in our example above would like help handling Kevin's disruptive behavior. They are hopeful that Kevin's dad can suggest effective strategies that have worked in the past to manage Kevin's behavior. At the same time, they are apprehensive that his dad may not respond well to their observations and questions. In their past experience with parents, the counselors expect that a dad might react in any of the following ways:

- Become defensive

- Blame the counselors (and/or the camp) for Kevin's behavior

- Make excuses for Kevin's behavior

▶ Be dismissive and minimize Kevin's actions

▶ Threaten and punish Kevin for his behavior

▶ Offer useful ideas that have worked in the past for Kevin

Any group leader would hope for the last reaction on this list! But, how do you increase the odds that parents will be open to your feedback about their child? When it comes to their own children, pragmatic parents can be emotional, even irrational in their reactions. But for most situations, the following methods will increase the likelihood that parents will be your allies rather than your foes.

① Think the best of all parents.

If you believe that the parents of your group members love their children and want the best for them in life, you will be much more likely to work effectively with them.

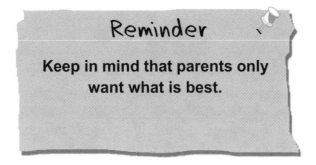

Reminder

Keep in mind that parents only want what is best.

Being a parent is not only an enormous responsibility, it can be pretty darn scary. I know. I have three kids myself. As much as I love and enjoy them, there is not a day that goes by that I don't worry about them. "Was Jesse able to talk to his math teacher about his homework?" "Did Lyana's friend snub her at recess this afternoon?" "Did Dov disrupt his P.E. class today?" In working with families for the past 20 years, I've learned that most parents are just like me. They are concerned about the welfare of their children, and they want them to grow up to be independent, happy adults. When I'm working with a parent who is angry, frustrated, or demanding, I remember that important point. Knowing what's underneath the behavior helps me handle a parent in a much more caring and sensitive way.

Fundamental Beliefs about Parents

▶ Parents love their children.

▶ Families have their strengths. You just need to find them.

▶ You can learn a lot from the kids' parents, and the parents can learn a lot from you.

▶ Parents want the best for their children.

▶ Parents want you to like and appreciate their kids.

▶ Parents are committed to nurturing and developing their children's personal growth.

▶ Parents want respect.

② Listen! Listen! Listen!

Listen first, talk later. You can't fully understand and appreciate a child until you listen first to the parent's point of view. Ask questions. Most parents want to tell you their perception of their child. As you listen, keep your mind open to new information. Parents share their concerns, but they also share what makes them proud of their child. Show parents through your body language and facial expressions that you are listening.

Ways to Show Parents You Are Listening

▶ Look them in the eyes.

▶ Nod your head in agreement.

▶ Say words like, "Oh," "Uh huh," "Wow!"

▶ Ask relevant questions.

3 Be proactive.

Parents do not like surprises. Nothing infuriates a parent more than getting no warning before a bad report card comes home, for instance. Nor do parents like learning of their child's misbehavior from another parent (or child) rather than from the group leader. Imagine if Kevin's dad learns from another parent that Kevin has been acting out at camp. By communicating with Dad quickly, the counselors may be able to stop behavior before it gets out of hand.

Kids can be pretty poor communicators, and parents like to be kept in the loop. Make sure to let the parents know what is happening in your group. By keeping parents informed, you clue them in to any potential problems before they become unmanageable. You also curtail accusations like, "Why didn't you tell me about the problem before?"

4 Plan ahead.

Before you talk to a parent about anything of import, make sure you plan ahead of time what you want to say and what you're hoping to accomplish with the conversation. Let the parent know in advance what you'd like to talk about, and set a meeting time to discuss the subject. It's not a good idea to talk to a parent when you don't have enough time and there are distractions. For example, talking to a parent in the carpool line or just before or after a game are not good times for these types of discussions. Instead, sit down with the parent, without their child present, so that you can calmly address the child's needs, and address any questions or concerns that might arise.

An important aspect of advance planning is doing research. If a parent has an issue that they want to discuss with you, learn as much as you can about the problem before the meeting. For example, if a parent wants to talk to you about a conflict that occurred between the kids when you were not present, talk to everyone involved prior to the parent meeting to increase your understanding of the event. The better informed you are, the more helpful you can be to the parents.

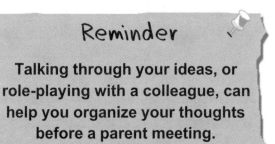

Reminder

Talking through your ideas, or role-playing with a colleague, can help you organize your thoughts before a parent meeting.

⑤ Accentuate the positive.

At the outset, let the parents know how much you care about and enjoy their child. All parents want to feel that their child is valued and in safe hands with a group leader. Begin the conversation by making positive comments about the child. Be specific with praise. Describe particular constructive behaviors that their child demonstrates and any progress the child is making in the group activity. In order to build a trusting, open relationship with you, a parent needs to know that you are on their kid's side.

Try Saying This:

"Mrs. McBride, I have seen so much growth in Clayton since the beginning of the school year. He is working particularly hard on his math facts. Have you noticed that at home?"

"Even though I know that we are here to talk about some of Kevin's behavior at camp, I have to tell you how much we enjoy Kevin's sense of humor. He makes us laugh every day."

"Thank you for taking the time to meet with me. Maureen is a pleasure to work with. She is a talented, dedicated musician who focuses completely during orchestra practice. She makes my job easy. I understand you have some concerns about my decision to remove her from first chair."

6 Communicate your needs directly.

State your needs clearly, calmly, and succinctly. Whether you are giving feedback to parents about their child's behavior or about their own behavior, make sure you communicate directly what you observe and how you would like for it to be different.

Try Saying This:

"I can see that you are out on the field every single game to support your son. You are his biggest fan out there. In your excitement, I'm not sure if you notice, but you are giving coaching directions to Sam at the same time that I am. He is looking pretty confused out there. I encourage you to keep on cheering for the team and for Sam, but I am asking that you stop coaching so that Sam can hear my directions. Can you do that for me?"

"Tiffany is having a very hard time following my directions. I'd really like to help her. What strategies have worked for you or other adults in her life to help her cooperate?"

"I can see how hard Kevin is trying to control his behavior with his fellow campers. He seems to get wound up and then can't bring himself back under control. We were thinking of trying to give him time-outs away from the group when we see him start to rev up. Have you ever used time-outs at home?"

---

7 Avoid defensiveness at all costs.

Even when you are the most positive communicator, you are going to hear parents complain to you. As the expression goes, "You can't please everyone." When faced with inevitable criticism, maintain your sense of calmness and a willingness to hear a parent out. Continue to watch your body language and facial expressions; your nonverbal behavior communicates just as loudly as your words. (Remember to use good communication skills discussed in the "Let's Talk" and the "Fighting Fairly" chapters of this book.)

Try Saying This:

(on the field) Parent: "Coach, I have a bone to pick with you. My son is sitting on the bench the whole game! What's the deal?"

Coach: "Mrs. Wilson, I'd like to talk to you about this. This isn't a good time. I'm too distracted and would like to hear what you have to say. I'll be in the gym tomorrow at 8 a.m. Can we meet for a few minutes then?"

_____

Parent: "I don't think you have very much control over your class."

Teacher: "I would really like to hear your concerns about this situation. Can we set a meeting time to talk about it further?"

_____

Parent: "Jeremy tells me that the kids in the class tease him and that he tells you, and you tell him not to tattle."

Teacher: "Tell me what you are hearing from Jeremy. Let's try to figure out what is going on here."

8 Use technology for communication.

If you have an email address or access to a website or bulletin board, you have a wonderful way to keep in touch with parents. Bulletin boards and websites can provide general information about programs, homework, and standards for behavior. Through regular emails, leaders and parents can update each other and track progress in a more efficient manner. Sometimes leaders are reluctant to initiate a dialogue with a parent through email or over the telephone. After you've had your initial meeting, these can be very effective ways to maintain continual contact.

Recently, I contacted my daughter's second-grade teacher, Ms. Crane, in response to a note on Lyana's report card. The note said that Lyana "needs improvement" in "using her time constructively." I wanted more information about my daughter's behavior so I emailed Ms. Crane, asking her if she could give me more details. I was so pleased with her response. She used the following strategies to communicate with me:

- ▶ She responded to my email immediately, which made me feel that she was taking my concern very seriously.

- ▶ She began her first paragraph by saying how much she loved having Lyana in her classroom and how well she was doing in school.

- ▶ In her second paragraph, she described the times of the day when Lyana had the most trouble organizing her activities – she would be looking around the room and talking with friends, thereby hindering her ability to manage her time.

- ▶ Ms. Crane went on to offer some strategies for helping Lyana at home as well as some techniques she uses in the classroom.

- ▶ She ended the email by thanking me for my inquiry and encouraging me to contact her at any time with further questions or concerns.

Didn't Ms. Crane handle this email communication beautifully?

⑨ Develop a plan.

End conversations with a plan so that each person understands what the next steps will be. Check in with each other at specific intervals to make sure that the plan is being implemented as agreed upon. If not, it may be useful to meet again to figure out what's getting in the way of meeting your goals.

Sample Plan

▶ The group leader will chart Kevin's off-task behavior on an hourly basis for a week to determine whether the behavior is related to time of day, specific activities, etc.

▶ The group leader will meet with the parent to discuss the findings of his observations by the end of next week.

▶ During this follow-up meeting, the group leader and the parent will develop a plan of action to help Kevin stay on-task.

By setting specific, achievable goals, the group leader is trying to establish a baseline to learn whether Kevin's off-task behavior is consistently high during certain times of the day or during specific activities. This information will help the group leader and the parents see if there is something in the environment that can be changed to help Kevin alter his behavior.

Parents can be great assets to the healthy functioning of your group. By establishing an open, collaborative relationship with parents, you set the stage for positive interactions to take place within the group.

Quirky Kids
Appreciating the Socially Awkward Child

Eric wondered how this camping trip was going to go for Ryan. Ryan was not like the other ten-year-old kids in his Boy Scout troop. During meetings, while the other boys laughed and joked with each other, Ryan kept to himself and seemed to prefer to be alone, taking apart his watch and putting it back together again. When spoken to, he would talk excitedly about watches, but rarely talked about anything else. The other boys in the group were not unkind to him, but they didn't go out of their way to include him either. Ryan's dad came to most of the meetings and encouraged his son to participate in the activities. Ryan cooperated when coaxed, but had a lot of trouble interacting appropriately with the other kids. When he did speak, he frequently blurted out irrelevant information. He seemed oblivious, even disinterested in what the other boys were doing. One time, another boy, Josh, fell and hurt himself right in front of Ryan, and Ryan just walked right by him as if he didn't notice.

Eric was relieved when Ryan's dad decided to come on the camping trip. He wasn't sure how to help Ryan feel more a part of the group. Because of this discomfort, Eric tended to let Ryan's dad take the lead on managing him. Eric felt guilty about passing off his responsibilities to Ryan's dad, but he was really at a loss for knowing how to engage a kid as quirky as Ryan.

We all remember a quirky kid from our childhood — the classmate who seemed completely ignorant of the rules of social etiquette. I very clearly remember a classmate of mine when I was in the fifth grade. Everybody thought he was weird. He would spend recess walking around the periphery of the playground. When my classmates and I tried to talk to him or play with him, he would ignore us. I remember him being an exceptional math student, way ahead of the rest of us. At the same time, he either couldn't (or wouldn't) read or write. At first, my peers and I were perplexed by him. As time went by, however, we gave up trying to figure him out and left him alone to circle the playground.

Now I know that this child probably had Asperger's Syndrome. In the last few decades, Asperger's has exploded into our consciousness. Sometimes referred to as high-functioning autistics, and sometimes fondly described as just plain quirky, kids with Asperger's lack social skills, have a limited ability to engage in a reciprocal conversation, and demonstrate an intense absorption in specific subjects (which may not be of interest to anyone else besides themselves). Seemingly unaware of the rules of social conduct, these quirky kids inadvertently offend their peers' feelings. They have few genuine friends and seem virtually unable to read people's body language. Parents of these children describe them as being socially isolated at best, and sometimes socially abused and rejected by peers.

Quirky kids do not learn the way other children learn. Like my fifth-grade classmate, they may find complex math equations a breeze to figure out, but are terribly confused by even the most basic verbal and nonverbal communication. Despite the disruptions to their social learning, however, these kids can gradually learn more appropriate codes of social conduct, often through intellectual analysis and instruction rather than natural intuition.

As a leader of children's groups, you will most certainly come in contact with children like Ryan. It's imperative that you help them have a positive experience with their peers. You're in a unique position to help them build skills and expand upon their social success. Their social gains may be slow and incremental, but they can occur.

Let's take a closer look at some of the interpersonal challenges these children exhibit.

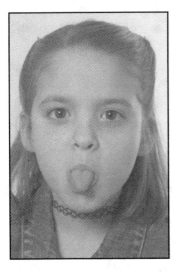

Quirky Kid Behavior

Insensitivity to the Social Signals and Feelings of Others

Human beings are constantly communicating with each other through verbal and nonverbal means. When we are hurt, we cry. When we are happy, we smile. When we are annoyed, our facial expression shifts to express our irritation. Social success requires a continuous scanning of our environment for clues that guide our social actions. Quirky children have tremendous difficulty tuning in to their social surroundings and then responding appropriately. The ability to empathize and understand the world from another person's perspective is a highly complex skill that they have difficulty mastering.

When Ryan walked past Josh, the boy who fell down in front of him, his behavior reflected his inability to feel and then respond empathically to a peer. Instead of focusing on Josh's welfare, Ryan was preoccupied with his own needs.

Lack of Awareness of Personal Body Space

Perhaps because the feelings of others are not recognized, quirky kids are unaware of the impact their actions might have on others. The lethal combination of impulsivity and lack of awareness of others' personal body space may lead people to view the quirky kids as deliberately rude, irresponsible, and even aggressive at times. It's important to understand that if these kids do behave aggressively, it is unlikely that the behavior is purposeful, i.e., done with the intent of hurting someone. For example, children with poor boundaries might grab things away from another child, without being aware that the object is in the hands of this child.

Self-Centeredness

Because they have difficulty seeing things from another's perspective, a child with these issues is self-centered. We show that we are focused outside ourselves by listening to others, waiting patiently while others finish speaking, and offering words of support when needed. Self-centeredness reflects self-sufficiency, a lack of need for outside approval. Selfishness, on the other hand, indicates an intentional focus on the self at the expense of others. Both Ryan and my fifth-grade classmate were self-sufficient to the point of avoiding social connection altogether.

Difficulty Sustaining Eye Contact

Eye contact is a basic building block to reading social signals and creating positive social interactions. "The eyes are the windows to the soul," as the saying goes. Through our eyes, we communicate so much about our mental state and our feelings. If a child does not look, he cannot see. When he doesn't look others straight in the eye, he is often viewed as untrustworthy, disinterested, and disconnected. Kids are drawn to those who make them feel good about themselves by looking at them and listening. Connection is limited if eye contact is not established. Kids with social issues often struggle in this very basic arena.

Bookish, Overly Formal Speech

Frequently delivered in a wooden, even robotic manner, the stodgy speech of some quirky kids is tolerated, even appreciated by some adults. Children, on the other hand, are not so enamored of this behavior. Peers may react to the academic vocabulary and rigid demeanor as intentional snobbishness. Peers don't understand that the emotional realm of feelings, with its associated range of facial expressions and varied vocal tones and cadences, is uncharted territory for many of these kids. Quirky kids may feel most safe and comfortable when they are focused on their own topic of special interest. With Ryan, it's clocks. When he describes clocks excitedly, using extremely precise language, it's not his intention to act like a know-it-all in front of his fellow Scouts. On the contrary, Ryan is communicating to others about what interests him, pure and simple. He's not able to anticipate the negative reactions he might receive from his peers.

Difficulty with Give-and-Take in Conversation

Conversation is like a game of catch. The speaker throws the ball to a listener; the listener catches the ball by using active listening words. The listener then throws the ball back by asking a question that expresses interest, or by making a statement that shows understanding. In order to have a satisfying game of catch, the ball needs to go back and forth between listener and speaker several times. Particularly in a group setting where many voices are interacting, the quirky kid will have trouble processing the information and responding, as spoken words and corresponding thoughts collide.

Strategies for Working with Quirky Kids

Despite the disruptions these children have in their social learning, they can improve their relationships with peers by gradually learning codes of conduct. With a little sensitivity on your part, the quirky kid can have a successful experience in a group. These are some ways that you can help:

1   Take the time to explain the rules of the game.

These kids frequently don't understand or care about the rules and goals of games and activities. Take time to break down the rules of play into simple steps. For instance, if you are playing a game of kickball, you might say the following:

Try Saying This:

"Ryan, when the ball comes to you, kick it as hard as you can. After you kick the ball, run as fast as you can to the white square with the number one on it. Put your foot on the square. When another teammate kicks the ball, you run to the square with the number two on it…"

You may need several attempts at explaining before the quirky kid becomes comfortable with the game. It may seem obvious to you that you run to the bases after you kick the ball, but this child needs to be taught the concept.

② Encourage taking the other child's perspective.

Rarely does the quirky kid intend to hurt another child's feelings. You may need to help him understand the impact he has on others. Consistently ask him to explain how the other person may feel as a consequence of what he said or did.

You've heard the expression, "Act 'as if'." Even if the quirky child doesn't really understand or feel the nuances expressed by others, it's still important that he responds *as if* he understands. For instance, you can teach him simple words like "Oh" (said in a disappointed tone), to express empathy.

Try Saying This:

You: "Ryan, how do you think Josh felt when he fell down, and you didn't ask if he was all right?"

Ryan: "I don't know."

You: "Ryan, when another child falls down and gets hurt, the right thing to do is ask, 'Are you all right?' to show that you are concerned."

Ryan: "Oh, okay."

We are constantly prompting the children in our *Stepping Stones* groups. These simple prompts help the kids say and do the right thing, even if they don't necessarily understand why it's the right thing.

③ Continue to use praise and discipline effectively.

Understanding that a child is unique does *not* mean that you don't apply appropriate discipline. Set clear limits with *all* of the kids you work with, including the quirky kids. Make sure that you give commands clearly and firmly, and impose an immediate consequence if a command is not followed.

Be extra certain that the child is attuned to you before you give the command. Once I gave a command to one of my quirky group members, and he ignored it, so I had to repeat myself. I realized too late that he was not listening to me. He was surprised by the consequence that followed the warning and he became extremely upset and tearful – it took several minutes to calm him down. I certainly learned from this episode, and in the future made sure he was paying attention to me before I asked him to do something.

Try Saying This:

"Ryan, I see that you're dressed for the day, but now you need to put your pajamas back in your duffel bag."

If your direction is not followed, say:

"You have not put your pajamas back in your duffel bag. For each minute I wait for you to do what I asked, you will lose a minute of 'clock dismantling' time."

Just as with consequences for misbehavior, praise needs to be immediate as well. Be specific with your praise. For instance:

"Ryan, I really like that you put your pajamas back in your duffel back as soon as you were dressed for the day – even without my asking you to!"

④ Be careful how you handle the quirky kid's mistakes.

Kids who are different are frequently rejected by peers. This social isolation often results in low self-esteem and an intense fear of making mistakes, which makes it very difficult for these kids to take chances. In the minds of these kids, one mistake is just as enormous as the next. If Ryan sees all of his mistakes as huge, he may choose to retreat into his own world, rather than face possible failure whenever he ventures outside of it.

You can help a child work through this fear of failure by making certain that you react calmly to his mistakes. If he makes a mistake, try to show him alternative behaviors that would correct for the mistake. Continually encourage all your group members to take risks, and then praise them for their efforts to do so.

Try Saying This:

"I'm glad to see you here. I know that the last camping trip was hard for you. I am confident that this time you will enjoy yourself!"

"Everyone strikes out some of the time. The important thing is to try to make a hit next time you're up at bat!"

"We all get mad and do things that we regret. Here is a bucket with water, soap, and a brush. If you scrub hard enough, you'll get that marker off the wall."

⑤ Model self-disclosure and ask lots of leading questions.

Because kids like Ryan have a lot of difficulty appropriately expressing and identifying feelings, it's important that you continually self-disclose.

Try Saying This:

"I feel disappointed that we lost the game."

"I'm frustrated that I can't find my shoes."

"I'm so excited about our next activity."

"I'm sad that he dropped off the team."

In addition, ask a lot of leading questions that will help the child identify his own feelings and emotional reactions throughout the day.

Try Saying This:

"Did you feel excited during our camping trip today?"

"Did you feel disappointed that it rained today?"

"I bet you were frustrated when you couldn't hit the ball?"

"Were you unhappy that we had hot dogs instead of hamburgers for dinner?"

Reminder
Quirky kids need help experiencing and expressing gradations of emotion. For instance, allow the child to rate his level of upset from 1 to 10.

6 Make direct statements.

Quirky kids tend to have great difficulty decoding and integrating nonverbal clues and messages. When Ryan's fellow troop member, Josh, fell and hurt himself, his facial expression communicated pain and upset. Josh might even have been crying. But Ryan had no idea that Josh's facial expression was indicating upset. If he had known that Josh needed help, Ryan would have helped him. Ryan's apparent lack of empathy and compassion really stems from his nonverbal language deficit. Ryan cannot interpret or understand facial expressions and body language. That's why direct comments and requests are the best form of communication to use with these kids.

Deliver information in a concrete manner. When words are not effective, you can develop hand signals with the child, or even flash cards to communicate requests.

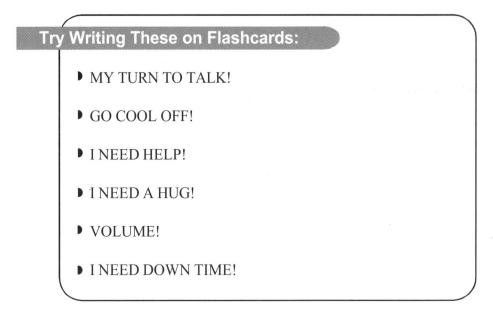

Try Writing These on Flashcards:

▶ MY TURN TO TALK!

▶ GO COOL OFF!

▶ I NEED HELP!

▶ I NEED A HUG!

▶ VOLUME!

▶ I NEED DOWN TIME!

7 Make the parent your ally.

Parents of quirky kids are generally very aware of their child's social issues and are keenly sensitive to the social isolation and rejection their children face. You need to be especially sensitive to the feelings of both the child and his parents. It's important to take the time to strategize with the parents on different ways to make the group safe and comfortable for the child.

Try Saying This:

"I notice that Ryan tends to stay on the sidelines. In the past, how have you been able to get him involved?"

"Tell me how I can be most helpful to your son."

"What do I need to know about your daughter to make this experience work for her?"

8 Watch out for the "scapegoat"!

When things go wrong, we do not like to blame ourselves. So, we often look for a scapegoat on whom we can dump our misplaced anger and aggression. Children pick on kids who are different and/or unable to resist or fight back. Quirky kids make ideal scapegoats for this reason. Don't let anyone in your group scapegoat anyone else. If you notice it occurring with those who are unable to fight back, you must be even more hyper-vigilant on behalf of the victim.

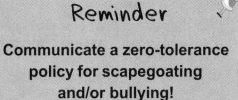

Reminder

Communicate a zero-tolerance policy for scapegoating and/or bullying!

Sometimes quirky kids behave in unpredictable ways. For instance, when they feel anxious, they may react by giggling. At times, the giggling may seem to come out of nowhere. The child may be reacting to a thought that just crossed his mind or a particular word that strikes him as funny. When this happens, peers become confused. This situation can easily lead to bullying.

Although quirky kids do present unique challenges for the group leader, they can be fascinating children who think very differently than we do. As group leaders, we always learn the most from the children who test us. Quirky kids offer us a great opportunity to discover new ideas and strategies in our work as group leaders.

Raising Kids' Self-Esteem
Building Confidence

Spencer is a small, shy boy with a sad face who carries himself as if he has the weight of the world on his shoulders. When he participates in group activities, and the other kids are nice to him or compliment him, Spencer is unable to accept their kindness. He tends to put his head down and wander off rather than say the simple "thanks" that is required. Spencer feels he has no friends and that nobody in his group likes him. He also feels helpless to do anything about this and is unaware of the many talents (e.g., computer skills, video game aptitude) he could bring to a friendship with other 10-year-old boys.

Much research has been done focusing on the importance of high self-esteem to a child's emotional development. You may already know that self-esteem is vital, but you may not know how to help a child develop high self-esteem. This chapter focuses on how self-esteem affects the quality of a child's peer relationships and how you, as a leader, can help your kids feel good about themselves. Once a child has acquired high self-esteem, it's much easier for him to establish the kind of friendships he needs. "You can't love others until you love yourself" is as true for friendship as it is for love. "You can't have a friend until you are a friend."

What is Self-Esteem?

The kids I work with give these definitions of self-esteem: "It's how we feel about ourselves." "If you have self-esteem, you like yourself." "I'm okay, so I have it." When we think about self-esteem, we usually think about it in terms of thoughts and feelings about ourselves. What we sometimes forget is that self-esteem also refers to feelings of competency and control.

Children with low self-esteem do not feel empowered; they feel that no matter what they do, they can't make a difference. If good things happen to kids with low self-esteem, they believe it was a fluke. When bad things happen to them, they think it was bad luck or someone else's fault.

For example, a child with low self-esteem might say,
> "I only caught that fly ball because it came right to me."

A child with high self-esteem would say,
> "I caught that fly ball because I've been practicing a lot."

A child with low self-esteem and difficulty making friends might say,
> "All the kids are mean to me because they are jerks!"

A child with high self-esteem who has the same peer problems would say instead,
> "Gee, I wonder how I could change my behavior so that others will like me."

Kids with little self-assurance will make different social choices than children who believe in themselves. Those with low self-esteem tend to choose others with poor self-esteem. These choices have consequences, which can further lower self-esteem. And so the cycle continues.

Kids with High Self-Esteem:

- Have a relaxed and balanced posture

- Maintain good eye contact with others

- Have alert and bright eyes

- Socialize well with others

- Have good personal hygiene

- Have friends with high self-esteem

- Are realistically aware of their strengths and limitations

- Can accept rejection or critical feedback

- Can say "no" to peers

- Set small goals and achieve them

- Are able to tune into other people's needs

- Have "stick-to-it-ness"

- Have fairly stable moods

Kids with Low Self-Esteem:

- Often blame others for their own actions

- Might speak too loudly or too softly

- Need to be liked by everyone

- See themselves as losers

- Are critical of others

- Have trouble making and keeping friends

- Have difficulty accepting compliments

- Have trouble accepting responsibility for their actions

- Get frustrated easily

- Make negative comments about themselves

- Tend to be quitters

- May brag

- Can be bullies

Raising Your Kids' Self-Esteem

The following steps will help you create a safe and nurturing environment in which your kids can develop high self-esteem. Please keep in mind a child's unique temperament when practicing these techniques.

① Encourage areas of competence.

Help your children find their "areas of competence" as stepping stones on the road toward high self-esteem. Support them in finding their strengths (sports, computers, music, drama, and so on) and encourage involvement in these activities. If a child struggles in areas that society highly values, such as school or playing team sports, he may feel tremendous self-doubt. Children need to experience a sense of accomplishment to feel good about themselves. It's up to you to help your kids discover their areas of competence and reinforce those strengths.

Spencer, in the example above, may not be a talented athlete, but he does have his *own* talents. Many children are like Spencer. They minimize their own strengths and compare themselves negatively to others.

② Promote physical fitness.

Regardless of a child's particular areas of competence, physical activity must be a part of a child's normal routine. If a child is opposed to playing team sports, that's okay. How about horseback riding? Or martial arts? Or bike riding?

③ Find ways during the day to encourage self-esteem.

Anytime you see a group member do something well, let him know. Having led children's groups for the last 20 years, I can feel pretty burnt out on some days. My viewfinder becomes focused on the negative aspects of the kids in my group. I can't help myself. It is at those times that it's most important for me to emphasize the positive in my kids. When you slide down that inevitable slope of impatience and negativity, catch yourself. Find something positive to say to one of your kids or to the group as a whole. Doing this makes everybody in the group, including you, feel a whole lot better.

④ Encourage independence.

Listen carefully when a child tells you about his problems. Avoid answering

questions too quickly. Let a child struggle a little to find his own solutions.
Allow him to make choices.

Frequently, kids will dump their problems into an adult's lap with words
like, "I can't do this," or "I made a mistake, you need to make it right." We
adults do a disservice to children when we play the hero and jump in to fix
their problems at every turn. Instead, it's important to allow kids to think
things through on their own. The kids may want you to fix it, but they don't
need you to fix it. There's a difference. When children work things through
on their own with our empathic support, they feel empowered. This leads to
greater self-esteem.

Try Saying This:

"Which activity do you want to attend?"

"Who do you want to buddy with this afternoon?"

"I'm not sure how to answer that question. Why don't you
think about it for a bit and see what you come up with."

"Which one of these problems do you want to work on first?"

Allow kids to do things for themselves. Assume that they can complete
tasks without your help, and most of the time they will surprise you.

5 Encourage positive self-talk.

Perhaps you've heard a child say things like, "I stink at this," "I can't do
this," or "I hate myself." These words perpetuate feelings of hopelessness.
When a child is experiencing an emotional situation, the thoughts that go
through his head can be either helpful by urging him forward, or hurtful by
holding him back. A child who says negative things to himself is not going to
soothe himself; rather, his words will stir him to new heights of anger.

Give your kids new language to use during difficult times.

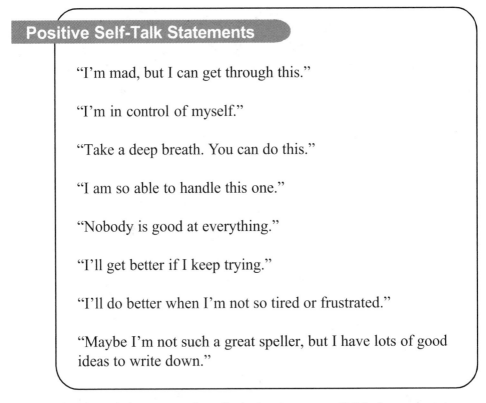

Positive Self-Talk Statements

"I'm mad, but I can get through this."

"I'm in control of myself."

"Take a deep breath. You can do this."

"I am so able to handle this one."

"Nobody is good at everything."

"I'll get better if I keep trying."

"I'll do better when I'm not so tired or frustrated."

"Maybe I'm not such a great speller, but I have lots of good ideas to write down."

You've heard the expression, "mind over matter." It's important to encourage your kids to stay focused and positive so that they can accomplish their goals. Listen to any negative self-statements and then respond positively.

6 Provide opportunities for self-monitoring.

A basic component of high self-esteem is the ability to observe ourselves and to change our behavior to fit the demands of a particular situation. To encourage this ability, you can provide opportunities for your kids to observe their own behavior and then make decisions about how to proceed.

7 Help the kids appreciate and accept differences in others.

Remember that your group members will directly pick up your level of tolerance and willingness to include others. Be careful what you say in front of them. This may seem obvious, but if you have strong negative feelings toward someone else, your kids will tend to pick up on that and mirror your sentiments.

Reminder

You are a role model for your group. Make sure you communicate the right message.

8 Encourage your kids to socialize with other children who have high self-esteem.

Make sure your group members are involved in many extracurricular activities, especially during adolescence. Encourage them to befriend others with similar interests. In my experience, kids with high self-esteem tend to engage in healthy peer relationships. Their self-confidence gives them the ability to evaluate situations objectively and to make appropriate judgments about them.

9 Help your kids learn from mistakes.

Kids with low self-esteem are terribly afraid of making mistakes. And this fear makes it very difficult for them to take chances. It also can make it hard for them to follow through with activities. Instead, they become quitters because they're afraid they won't perform the activity perfectly. You can help a child get over the fear of failure, although it's not an easy task. Try the following:

Handling Mistakes

▶ Bring attention to your own mistakes.

▶ React calmly when you make mistakes. Allow your kids to see how you handle errors. Speak out loud about the mistakes you make and how you learn from them.

▶ React calmly to a child's mistake. Don't say demeaning things like, "I told you it wouldn't work," "That was not a smart thing to do," or "You weren't thinking straight." Instead, say out loud, "I bet we can learn something from this," or "Don't worry. Everyone makes mistakes."

▶ Always focus on what children do well rather than on what they don't do well.

▶ Talk about your own childhood blunders. Discuss how you lived through them and what you learned from them.

Regardless of how high a child's self-esteem is, the above strategies can significantly increase his feelings of competence. There are also games and exercises that can help boost a child's self-esteem. Give them a try!

Self-Esteem Games and Exercises

Thinking Straight and Feeling Great!

This exercise is designed to help your kids see a potentially negative situation in a new light. Have your kids choose a situation that makes them feel badly. Try to help them change negative thoughts to positive ones by talking through a situation using the following questions.

Positive Self-Talk Worksheet

What am I thinking about this situation?

_____

_____

_____

Which thoughts are negative thoughts?

_____

_____

_____

What are some positive thoughts about the situation?

_____

_____

_____

What is my new way of feeling about this situation?

_____

_____

_____

Say Something Positive - Candy Game

Equipment: M & M's or other candy

(Make sure no one in the group has an allergy to nuts. Also, if anyone knows the game, ask them not to give it away.) Have a supply of M & M's to share with the group. Ask the group to sit in a circle. Pass the M & M's around and ask each member to take as many as they need. Don't tell the kids what they'll need the candy for. You'll notice that some of the kids will take a few, and some will take *a lot*! Then, ask the group members to state out loud a personal strength for each M&M they took.

Say Something Positive - Fill the Jar with Positives

Place a jar of checkers or marbles in the middle of a table, perhaps during a meal. Ask each child to make positive statements about himself. Every positive statement is rewarded with a checker. The winner is the one with the most checkers at the end.

Say Something Positive - Fill in the Blanks

Ask your group to write down the answers to these questions.

I am proud of:

_____

_____

_____

Things that I would like to change about myself are:

_____

_____

_____

Accomplishment Scavenger Hunt

Hand out the following list to everyone. Each participant must go around during the day and write down others' names next to the accomplishments he observes.

▶ Has been nice to a friend

▶ Was a member of a team sport

▶ Faced a fear alone

▶ Told someone how he felt

▶ Won a prize or award

▶ Made a mistake and learned from it

▶ Tried a new activity even though it was hard for him

List of Strengths

Begin a list of your group members' strengths. Leave the list out in a visible place, and add to it daily as you witness your kids' positive attributes.

Stop It!!

Develop a signal with your kids to help them stop negative thoughts. For instance, say you choose together the code word "Shazam." Whenever any one of the kids says something negative about himself, you say "Shazam" to signal him to change his thoughts.

I Think I Can

Make "I think I can" signs. Post them in multiple places to help the kids remain positive. Here are some suggested phrases:

I Can Do It!	I'm Cool!
I Know I Can!	I Care!
Just Do It!	Keep On Trying!
I Deserve It!	Don't Give Up!

Social Skills Coaching
Encouraging Healthy Friendships

Scout Leader Andy can't help noticing that a couple of the boys in his Cub Scout Troop have highly developed leadership skills. Andre and Tim, in particular, have a way of getting the boys to rally around them. They show a keen sense of awareness of the dynamics in the group, and can mediate conflicts between their fellow troop members better than most adult leaders. Both Andre and Tim intuitively know when it's appropriate to kid around and when it's time to focus on the activity at hand. Andy wishes all of the boys were able to conduct themselves in group the way that these boys can. Unfortunately, while there are some kids who get along just fine with the other kids, very few show the same kind of social expertise as Tim and Andre. And then there are others who don't seem to understand their peers at all. Some of these boys stand on the sidelines and just watch, unable to find a way into the group. And then there are others who barrel head first into the social interactions, unaware of the social wreckage they're causing. Andy wants to help the boys improve their social skills, but he doesn't know how.

Social Skills Can Be Learned

Good social skills enable children to get along well with others and build friendships with peers. In many children's groups, the social skills necessary to make and keep friends can be learned. And in the long run, children with good social skills will experience future successes in any social situation. All kids can raise their "Social IQ." And, you as their group leader are in an ideal position to guide them toward that goal.

Kids with a high social IQ are those who 1) interact easily and well with others; 2) actively listen when spoken to; 3) resolve conflicts using nonviolent means; and 4) possess a high self-esteem. They instinctively understand what is expected, and can effortlessly size up a social situation. These kids can smoothly join a group of children playing and "go with the flow." In general, these children can follow others' good examples, so when parents and peers behave in socially appropriate ways, the socially adept child automatically learns from them and internalizes the lessons.

Children like Andre and Tim in the story above have high social IQ's. It is the rare child who naturally displays all of these skills, however. Most kids need to learn good interpersonal interaction skills and need guidance and mentoring to do so. As group leaders, you can help your kids raise their social IQ. Group settings are the perfect place to engage children socially and teach skills for positive social interactions. Groups frequently provide rich environments for kids to interact with peers, offering constant opportunities for negotiation, peaceful conflict resolution, and camaraderie building. However, without the strong leadership and caring encouragement of adults like you, healthy friendships within the group may not happen.

Becoming a Social Skills Coach

Many of the strategies and pointers in this chapter grew out of my work developing and implementing the *Stepping Stones* social skills program. This program specifically addresses the needs of the socially challenged child. Through years of observation and experience, I've learned from the *Stepping Stones* kids what skills they need help developing and how to approach building these skills in a unique way.

As a group leader, you already help your kids develop social skills by modeling good social skills yourself and by creating situations in which your group members can practice these skills. For example, every time you encourage a child to participate in an activity or collaborate in a particular game or sport, you are helping him build social skills.

In order to be most effective in this role, you must first acquire expertise as a social skills coach. Listed below are some basic guidelines and goals for you to follow. Your role as social skills coach requires you to wear several different hats, some of which will be new and unfamiliar to you.

Set Goals for Yourself

- Be enthusiastic! Enjoy yourself!

- Learn group members' names quickly.

- Communicate that each member is important, accepted, and secure.

- Know your audience. Before you choose your curriculum, exercises, or activities, find out if any of the kids already know one another so that you can be tuned in to any group dynamics. Determine the group's cognitive, emotional, and physical capabilities.

- Create an atmosphere that is safe and nonjudgmental.

▶ Be flexible and spontaneous. If you don't think an exercise or game is working, be prepared to change it at a moment's notice.

▶ Encourage basic sharing and communication. You want the kids to get to know one another better and make friends; it's that simple.

The basic training methods below work well in helping kids get along well with one another and make friends. Try them out!

1 Model positive social behaviors.

"Modeling" means demonstrating for the kids how to perform a particular behavior. You are always modeling social skills, without even knowing it. For example, when you take turns, cooperate with others, "go with the flow," and say "please" and "thank you," you are modeling positive social skills for your kids.

The kids look to you for clues as to how they should behave or respond to a situation. For many children with an innately high social IQ, this "passive" modeling is sufficient to help them learn what they need to know to get along with others.

2 Prompt the kids to use good social skills.

There are many opportunities for your kids to use their social skills in a group setting. They may not always remember to use them, however. Your job is to gently, but firmly, remind the kids to use their skills. You won't need to prompt them as much in the moment if you can anticipate with them situations when their skills are going to come in handy, and discuss them with the kids ahead of time.

Try Saying This:

"Isaac, remember we talked before about taking turns?"

"Emma, remember how we learned to settle arguments?"

"Brad, remember your goal is to sit at lunch with your friend, Brian."

Reminder

Be firm when prompting, but do not use an angry tone of voice because you do not want to embarrass or discourage a child's efforts.

Another way to prompt privately is to arrange together a nonverbal cue that only you and your group member understand. For instance, you could pull on your ear to tell the child his voice is too loud. This allows the child to alter his behavior in response to your cue without embarrassing him in front of his fellow group members.

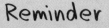 3   Practice and rehearse social skills.

Practicing social skills is like practicing a musical instrument or a sport. Everyone needs to practice, but different levels of natural talent will require different levels of effort. Children with a lower social IQ are going to require more frequent and consistent practice. One way to rehearse is through role-play. Having the kids role-play the situation once or twice and then perform the skill in a real-life setting is helpful. Often times, kids need to role-play, then practice in a real-life situation, and then role-play again in order to learn and understand the skill. Even then, this cycle could repeat itself several times before the skill becomes more automatic. Like any other skill, it is the *practice* that actually gives a child the confidence he needs to perform the skill.

4 Reinforce interpersonal connections.

Our culture values independence and self-determination in youngsters. But these traits can lead to a decrease in a child's ability to identify and relate to the needs and feelings of others. Independence and connection are not mutually exclusive concepts. It's important that you help your kids value the opinions and desires of others so that they can develop lasting friendships and significant relationships with others. It is essential that they learn the elements of sharing in a group.

Elements of Sharing in a Group

> ▶ Everybody gets a chance to speak
>
> ▶ Listen while others are speaking
>
> ▶ No one raises their hand while another person is speaking
>
> ▶ Focus is on the speaker, not your own thoughts
>
> ▶ Show interest by asking questions, nodding, and saying "Uh Huh" or "Me, too!"

I have found it useful to post the Elements of Sharing list in a spot where everyone can refer to them easily. Sometimes the kids need gentle reminders to use their skills.

⑤ Encourage feedback from peers.

Peer feedback provides a powerful means for reinforcing skills. The kids learn how to lend support and offer constructive criticism to peers. Feedback can take the form of suggestions, opinions about how a child is impacting others in the group, coaching, and support. This type of performance feedback is effective, in part, because the observations are made by peers rather than adults. Kids care more about how their peers view them than their adult leaders. This is especially true with older children who are increasingly focusing their energy on developing and maintaining connections outside of adults. Your role is to coach the kids on how to offer feedback appropriately.

Teaching Social Skills in the Outdoors – The S.O.A.R. Approach

Some of you have the opportunity to work with kids outdoors. This gives you a great opportunity to integrate social skills training into your everyday games and activities.

A unique training method that we use in our *Stepping Stones* outdoor social skills training groups is the S.O.A.R. approach:

   S –   **Stop action**

   O –   **Observe aloud**

   A –   **Ask for feedback**

   R –   **Reinforce the skill**

Using this technique, you can highlight specific social interactions (both negative and positive) that you observe in the group. For example, using this method, a leader who notices two boys having a heated disagreement can freeze the interaction while the kids in the group use the S.O.A.R. method. Let's take a look at how this example would play out.

S – (Stop action)	The altercation is frozen.
	Leader: "Okay, guys, freeze!"
O – (Observe aloud)	You ask the group what they see happening between the boys. In this way, the group defines the problem between the boys and allows them the necessary distance from the conflict.
	Leader: "What do you see going on here between Devin and Marco?"
A – (Ask for feedback)	You ask the group for ideas to solve the problem.
	Leader: "Both Devin and Marco want to play with the video game now. What do you think they could do to solve this conflict?"
R – (Reinforce the skill)	You highlight the skills the group demonstrates, e.g., positive conflict resolution skills, appropriate problem solving, and anger management skills.
	Leader: "Those were all great ideas. I think we have all learned something today. By thinking positively and being open to several possible solutions, Devin and Marco were able to reach a solution without damaging their friendship."

By using the S.O.A.R. approach in this situation, the two boys are able to get "unstuck" from their conflict. Although Devin and Marco are initially reluctant to accept suggestions from their peer group, with the support of the group they are able to ultimately achieve compromise and move forward.

It's not necessary to use S.O.A.R. only when a conflict exists. You can also freeze action with your kids any time you witness appropriate social interactions. For instance, try stopping action when your kids are demonstrating good sportsmanship skills on the ball field.

S – (Stop action)

Leader: "Hey, guys, let's freeze for a second here."

O – (Observe aloud)

Leader: "Is anyone else noticing what great sportsmanship I'm seeing on the field today? I'm sure you have all witnessed examples of good sportsmanship today. Can anyone give me an example?"

A – (Ask for feedback)

Leader: "What is it like to have your fellow campers cheer you on? If you like it, yell 'YES'!"

R – (Reinforce the skill)

Leader: "This group has shown terrific teamwork today!"

Keep in mind, this technique takes some getting used to. The kids will initially resent the interruption of their activities. Typically, however, once they catch on to the idea, they understand the benefits of looking more closely at themselves and their relationships within the group. This here-and-now approach views interaction through a magnifying glass at the moment it happens, rather than examining the behavior after the fact when interventions lose their immediacy and relevance. This phenomenon of working in the moment is one of the great benefits of group work in general.

The S.O.A.R. approach allows kids to:

- Find new ways to handle stressful situations

- Take responsibility for actions

- Walk in another person's shoes

- Improve self-esteem

- Encourage self-awareness

- Express feelings with words rather than actions

With your guidance and coaching, your group will improve their interpersonal relationships and create more opportunities for friendships to develop.

Tough Questions
Kids Ask the Darndest Things

Melissa usually enjoys the time before bed when the 13-year-old girls in her bunk share personal stories. They talk about their families, their boyfriends, and their hometowns. The girls have lots of questions for each other. "Do you have a boyfriend? What's he like?" "What do you and your friends do for fun on the weekends?" "What kind of music are you into?" Through their conversation, more of their true selves emerge. Melissa is on "active duty" tonight – she is the night counselor. It's the night counselor who hears it all (whether she wants to or not!). This is Melissa's opportunity to take the pulse of her campers. She gets a solid view of the dynamics between the girls, hears what's on their minds, and what their lives are like outside of camp. She likes to sit back in the shadows and listen. The girls, on the other hand, want Melissa to be part of the discussion. At 20, Melissa is not that much older than her campers. They think she's cool. They see her as a big sister who can show them the ropes. With their intense curiosity come a lot of probing questions. "Do you have a boyfriend?" "Have you had sex with him?" "How far have you gone?" Melissa wants the girls to like and trust her, but she is really uncomfortable with their personal inquiries. Even though she's been a counselor for three years, she is still caught off guard by questions about her private life.

Kids ask the darndest things. How many times have you been caught off guard by a child asking a question that is a bit too personal? How do you respond to an inquisitive child who asks you about your past experience with sex, drugs, and rock n' roll? Have you ever gotten those "anxiety provoking" questions about death, terrorism, and natural disasters? Another favorite is the seemingly unanswerable question: "Is there a God?"

Although there is not a right or wrong answer to a child's probing inquiry, it may help you to know some basic strategies for handling these tough questions when they inevitably arise. Your capacity to respond appropriately helps the kids maintain an open, honest way of interacting with the world.

① Set your boundaries clearly and succinctly.

Answering personal questions can become a slippery slope, especially with teenagers. Personal questions are less likely to come up if you're a school teacher, a soccer coach, or a Girl Scout leader. But, if you're an overnight camp counselor – watch out! Part of what makes summer camp so special is the closeness that develops between campers and their counselors. Living in close quarters for days, sometimes weeks and months, re-

sults in an intimacy that is hard to replicate in the world outside of camp. This intimacy is a breeding ground for personal questioning. And, once you begin to answer personal questions, you'll find yourself barraged with more inquiries. Not only are teenagers curious, but they also enjoy testing limits. Many teens will push and push until they hit a solid wall. You can curtail this by setting your limits up front.

In the example above, Melissa might find it helpful to prepare in her mind a standard response when asked questions that catch her off guard. Once she is comfortable with giving her response, the kids will pick up on her comfort level and will be more likely to back off from asking personal questions.

Two topics of particular interest to kids are sex and drugs. In both cases, I strongly discourage you from revealing this kind of personal information about yourself to your group.

Try Saying This:

"I know you are curious about me, and I want to be here for you, but I am not comfortable talking about my personal life with campers."

"It's a camp rule that we counselors don't answer personal questions. I happen to agree with the rule."

"I'm glad you feel comfortable talking to me. I hope you know that you can talk to me about anything. However, I just can't go there when it comes to personal questions. That's where I feel I need to draw the line. So, what's up?"

Now that we have taken personal questions out of the equation, we can move on to how you can deal with other awkward questions as they arise.

2 Legitimize the question.

When a child respects your boundaries as an adult, it makes things much less complicated. However, there are some questions that are still difficult for the child to ask and for you to answer. It is absolutely crucial that you let the child know that you are a safe, understanding listener. This begins by letting the child know that any question is valid and worthwhile. No matter how unusual, surprising, or potentially embarrassing the question, the child needs to know that you will not reject it. All that's required for a supportive reaction is a smile and a simple response.

Try Saying This:

"That's a very good question. You are asking me…" (repeat the question as you heard it.)

"Many kids your age have asked me the same question."

"You're asking a very interesting question. Let me think about it…"

"You're not alone in wondering about this."

"I know this must have been tough for you to talk to me about. I'm glad you did."

③ Find out what they know.

Frequently, a child asks a question to seek reassurance. She may have heard bits and pieces about a topic, and is looking to you to fill in the blanks. So, if you can find out in a nonjudgmental way what she already knows about a subject, then you can ascertain how much information to provide to satisfy the need. Sometimes kids have inaccurate ideas, which can also be the source of unrealistic fears. When you can, try to give short-and-sweet information to a child. Answer on the child's level. Obviously, a four-year-old is going to require very different information than a twelve-year-old.

My immediate impulse when a child (or anyone, for that matter) asks me a question is to offer an answer. Even as a psychotherapist, group leader, and mother, I have trouble pausing long enough to figure out how to come up with a suitable response. I find that when I take even a few seconds to think a question through, my gut will usually tell me how to proceed. The words "Hmmm, let me think about that for a second" can be extraordinarily helpful in giving me the space I need to proceed appropriately.

Reminder

Be mindful and respectful of parental authority.

If a child doesn't have knowledge about a sensitive topic, like sex, perhaps the parents don't want their child to know about it. Kids should always be encouraged to talk to their parents or other family members first. Unfortunately, in many cases, kids don't feel they have anyone who will answer their questions in a nonjudgmental way. Instead, they get information from their friends, which is often inaccurate and misleading.

The following are a couple of ways to discover what a child knows about a subject before you attempt a response:

Try Saying This:

If a child asks, "Where do babies come from?" you can ask, "What do you think?"

If a child asks, "Are we going to be killed in a terrorist attack?" you can respond, "You seem quite concerned about a terrorist attack. What have you learned about terrorism at home and in school?"

If a child asks, "Can I catch AIDS?" you can answer, "I promise I will answer this question in the best way I can, but first I'd like to know what you know about AIDS."

④ Clarify the question before answering.

It seems so simple, doesn't it? Make sure you know what the child is asking before you answer. Sometimes, in an effort to be helpful, we launch into a reply before we even know the question. You can do this very simply by restating the question you heard. This communicates to the child that you are listening, and helps you make sure you've got the question right.

Try Saying This:

"Let me see if I understand you correctly. You are asking me if…"

"I'm hearing you ask…Am I on track?"

"Do I have this right? You want to know whether…"

"Okay. So you are telling me about …and you want to know…"

---

⑤ Understand the reason for the question.

Be aware that frequently, what is important about a question is not the question itself, but why it's being asked. Kids often ask questions because there's something deeper on their minds that they don't know how to express. They aren't always able to articulate their worries directly, so they may hide a question within a question. For instance, if a child asks you about sex, she may be trying to test your limits. If she's older, she may be attempting to understand her own feelings about the changes in her body. Be informative, but don't get too elaborate. Typically, it doesn't take much detail to quell a child's basic concerns.

6 Refrain from laughter or sarcasm.

If you can't quite deal with your own discomfort, that's okay. Take a deep breath and relax. But, whatever you do, don't resort to sarcasm or laughter! These common adult ways to diffuse tension only make kids feel humiliated.

7 Listen! Listen! Listen!

Have you ever noticed how quickly an upset child calms down after she has felt heard? Nothing feels better to a child (or an adult, for that matter,) than being heard. Kids frequently ask questions without really wanting an answer. Sometimes, they just want to know that you really listen. Give the kids in your group a chance to speak without judgment, and acknowledge their feelings.

Checklist for Active Listening

▶ Look directly at the child with a pleasant expression on your face.

▶ Keep your hands and body still.

▶ Don't interrupt.

▶ Periodically make sounds that express interest in what the child is saying, e.g., "Oh"; "Hmmm"; "Uh huh"; or "Oh yeah."

▶ Name the child's feelings with statements like, "Oh, that must have hurt," or "It's sad when a friend moves away."

8 If you are embarrassed, say so.

If kids sense that you are uneasy, they will feel the same way. Your unacknowledged embarrassment communicates to them that their question is inappropriate, or even bad. However, if you openly own your embarrassment, you're not putting this burden on the child. In addition, when you say out loud that you feel uncomfortable, it helps you feel less embarrassed. You could say something like, "This isn't easy for me to talk about. My parents never taught me how to answer tough questions like this. Let me see….."

9 If you don't know the answer, say so.

Don't feel that you have to have all of the answers to every question. There is absolutely nothing wrong with letting a child know that you don't have an immediate answer, but that you'll look into it and get back to them later.

Try Saying This:

"That's a great question! Let me think about it and get back to you."

"You know, I don't have the answer to that one right now. I'm going to check on it and get back to you tomorrow. Okay?"

10 Be honest.

Always be honest and reassuring. For instance, if a child tells you that she's afraid of dying, don't tell her that she's not going to die. Instead, you can acknowledge her anxiety while simultaneously stressing that death is a long way off.

Common Tough Questions

Safety

Recently, children have been bombarded with images of war, violence, and terror on TV, on the Internet, and in the newspaper. How can we best deal with their questions and relieve their concerns?

> ▶ **Monitor your own terrorism stress level.** Kids are emotional barometers. When significant adults in their lives exhibit signs of anxiety, they pick up on it and begin to express their own anxiety in both verbal and nonverbal ways.

> ▶ **Give clear and accurate answers.** It's much easier for kids to deal with factual information than with unknowns.

> ▶ **Don't overwhelm them by talking in-depth about the topic.** Kids younger than eight will get very little from a long discussion about war and terrorism.

> ▶ **Reassure the child that she is safe.**

> ▶ **Discourage violence as a way to manage conflict.** Encourage the kids in your group to find peaceful solutions to their everyday problems and conflicts.

Try Saying This:

"You are safe. The war is happening thousands of miles away."

"I can see why you would be scared about terrorism. But, we're lucky to live in this country where we are safe."

"I can tell you don't feel safe. Is there anything we can do together that would make you feel safer?"

Drugs/Alcohol

If you listen carefully to kids' questions about drugs and alcohol, you can hear that their feelings and concerns are the driving force behind the questions. You may need to help your kids distinguish between fact and fiction. If you can answer their questions in a factual manner, children are often satisfied.

Make sure that the information you provide is appropriate to the child's age and stage of development. For a child of seven or eight, you should focus on what is required to keep a body healthy and strong. You can also explain that smoking and taking medicines when we aren't sick is not healthy for our bodies.

An older child may want more specific information about drugs and alcohol. For example, a 13-year-old may want to know what marijuana looks like and how it affects people.

Reminder

You are a role model for your group. Make sure you communicate the right message.

In the teenage years, peer pressure is a major factor contributing to drug and alcohol use. Help your kids understand that a true friend is someone who respects your values and doesn't try to pressure you to change your feelings and decisions about using drugs or drinking alcohol.

Death

Kids are aware of death long before we realize they are. They experience death when autumn leaves turn brown and fall from the trees, or when they step over a dead bug. Death is a part of life that children strive to understand. Some of their questions about death may be stimulated by a TV show or a newspaper article and can be discussed in a fairly unemotional fashion.

There will be times when one of your kids has a personal experience with death. If she loses a relative, a friend, or even a pet, she may need to talk to an adult about her feelings. This adult may be you. Whenever a child in the group experiences a significant loss, the other kids frequently learn about it, and they may become anxious and upset themselves. They also may need a place to share their feelings and ask questions. These discussions can be difficult and heartbreaking for adults.

The following do's and don'ts will be helpful in answering children's questions about death:

Do's

- **Acknowledge that these questions are uncomfortable for you to answer.** This is typical, and the child appreciates your willingness to talk and listen.

- **Be aware of your own feelings about death so that when questions come up you are prepared to talk openly.**

- **Know that you don't have to have all the answers.** It's okay to say, "That's a tough one. I don't have the answer to that question."

- **Listen and accept the child's feelings.**

- **Try to keep your answers simple and short.** Don't overwhelm them with too many words. Kids will tune you out when you are saying too much.

- **Answer concrete questions in a concrete fashion.** For the question "What does dead mean?" use the answer, "A person who is dead can't breathe, or eat, and won't ever wake up."

- **Realistically reassure the child.** "Everybody dies. Most people are very old when they die. It is very unusual for a person to die young," and "No matter what, you will be taken care of."

▶ **Respond to a question with a question if it helps you understand the child's concerns more fully.** For instance, "What do you think happens after someone dies?"

▶ **Make sure that you let the child know that different people have different beliefs about death.** For instance, some people believe in heaven, some don't.

Don'ts

▶ **Don't use language that leads to misunderstanding.** For instance, avoid words such as "sleep," "on vacation," "went on a trip," or "rest" when describing death. As you can imagine, this leads to future anxiety when a parent travels, rests, or goes on vacation.

▶ **Don't use religion to explain death unless you have been asked by the family to do so.** Regardless of how strong or comforting your religious beliefs are to you, the child's family may not share them. It is also important for the child to accept the realities of death.

▶ **Don't make the child feel guilty or embarrassed about his curiosity.**

▶ **Don't scold a child for expressing feelings of anger or fear.**

▶ **Don't assume that all children grieve in the same manner.**

Answering questions about death may be difficult, even painful. If you prepare yourself for the possibility of questions about dying, you may find yourself playing a vital role as listener and mentor when the topic arises.

By nature, kids are curious beings. As a group leader, you become an important part of their lives. They may entrust you with their thoughts, feelings, and questions. Even when you are caught off guard, or feel uncomfortable, consider it an honor that you have built the trust necessary for them to be willing to ask you the tough questions.

Understanding Your Emotions
Knowing What Pushes Your Buttons

It was not the first time (or even the second) that Barbara had asked her sixth-grade students to settle down. She wondered why her class seemed especially noisy today. She had asked the students to split up into groups to brainstorm solutions to a social studies problem. Barbara was tired of disciplining them – she thought they were old enough to work together quietly. To make matters worse, Barbara was hungry. She had run out of the house before breakfast and skipped lunch to grade papers. Now she had a nagging headache that was not helping her mood. As the day progressed her students' voices got louder. They began to shout and argue with each other. She asked them once again to settle down as she thought to herself, "If I hear one more child talk above a whisper, I just might lose it." Then when she heard another argument ensue, she turned to the class and yelled, "That's it! What is the matter with you guys? I've told you far too many times to quiet down! You've all lost your recess today!!"

When you take on the enormous responsibility of managing groups of children, your buttons are going to be pushed. You're going to get upset with the kids from time to time – that's okay. But please don't confuse the unavoidability of your frustration as permission to lash out at the kids. Anger is a tricky emotion. Before you can expect your kids to manage their emotions effectively, you'd better be darn sure you can successfully handle your own.

Maintaining Your Emotional Calm

Emotional control is not automatic. However, understanding the factors that contribute to your feelings lessens the likelihood that outbursts will occur.

1 Know thyself.

The first step in expressing your emotions effectively is understanding what makes you more vulnerable to the challenging ones, like anger and frustration. For many of us, hunger and lack of sleep are two variables that lead to irritability. In Barbara's situation, perhaps she would have been less sensitive to her students' noise level if she had not skipped breakfast and lunch. If she had eaten nutritious snacks throughout the morning, would she have been as irritable in the afternoon? Perhaps not.

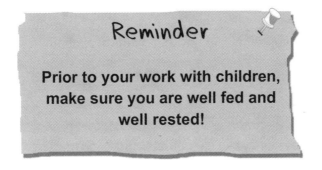

Reminder

Prior to your work with children, make sure you are well fed and well rested!

2 Minimize stress.

You may have heard the expression, "Stress at work leads to kicking the dog at home." There is truth to this. It is absolutely essential that prior to leading groups of children, you are aware of your own stress level. If you are under stress at work or at home, watch out for the danger signs of overreacting to common frustrations with kids. Like dogs, children can be easy targets during these times.

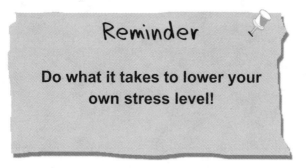

Do what it takes to lower your own stress level!

3 Let the kids know when you are stressed.

Don't hesitate to let the kids in your group know how you are feeling.

Try Saying This:

> "Hey guys, I am in a *really* bad mood today because I didn't sleep well last night. So, I'm asking you to keep your voices down today, okay?"

Children can sense when they need to handle you with kid gloves, so don't be afraid to communicate honestly with them about your needs.

4 Predict the outcome.

Before you set a standard of behavior for the kids, you must first know whether your expectations of them are reasonable, given their age and the nature of the situation. If you believe that they are, then make sure that you clearly define those expectations to the group in advance.

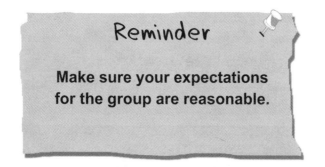

Make sure your expectations for the group are reasonable.

Try Saying This:

"Now we're going to break into four groups of six kids each. Your voices must be no louder than a whisper throughout this entire activity."

Anticipating events with kids allows them to make reasonable decisions regarding their own behavior. It also allows you to define for yourself what the boundaries are. If Barbara had told her students in advance about the consequences of their using loud voices, perhaps they would have chosen to be quieter.

Try Saying This:

"If you raise your voices, I will give you three warnings. After the third warning, we will have to stop the activity."

Reasonable consequences, clearly stated, lower the stress level in the classroom for both the student and the teacher.

5 Know your trigger thoughts.

Kids don't "make" you angry. Your thoughts and expectations do! Children are noisy, messy, and generally rather egocentric. They aren't particularly aware of other people's needs. And, they come in all kinds of different packages, some of which you'll like, and others you won't. Seeing children realistically will go a long way in helping you manage how you respond to them.

6 Maintain realistic expectations.

Whether you work with kids, or are raising them, pay attention to how much you use the word "should." Unrealistic expectations frequently accompany this word. "These kids *shouldn't* ask so many questions." "They *should* be better behaved." "Kids *should* know better." General awareness of children's social and emotional development at different ages will help you avoid having impractical expectations. Barbara was unrealistic about her chatty sixth-graders, thinking she could maintain peace and quiet during unstructured class time. She unwittingly set herself up for an angry outburst when her students failed to live up to her hopes for their behavior.

7 Change your thinking.

Loss of control almost always is the result of negative, escalating self-talk. Barbara became increasingly frustrated with her class when she thought to herself, "The kids are especially noisy today…I'm tired of disciplining the class…They should be able to work together quietly…If I hear one more child talk above a whisper." She might have been able to respond more calmly if she had paid more attention to the unconstructive nature of the thoughts going through her head. Once she was aware of her own pessimistic self-talk, Barbara could have tried to think more productive thoughts to cope with her unruly classroom.

Try Saying This to Yourself:

"I am feeling particularly sensitive to the noise today because I need to eat something."

"The kids are really into this assignment. That's why they are so loud and boisterous."

8 Assume bad behavior is unintentional!

Have you ever noticed that we are much more forgiving of bad behavior when we think it is accidental? It's when we attribute negative intent to a child's behavior that we become enraged. "He did that on purpose to get me mad!" "She is just trying to frustrate me!" Kids generally behave the way that they do to get their needs met. Whether they are looking for acceptance, attention, stimulation, or safety, children behave in a goal-directed manner. And, believe it or not, the goal is *not* to drive us crazy (although that may be the result.) Assuming that a child's behavior is deliberate does nothing to change it. Instead, presume all poor behavior is unintentional and see how much easier it is for you to solve problems rationally and consistently.

⑨ Apologize.

If you feel regrets about the way that you expressed anger, apologize to the kids. Be specific as possible in your apology. In Barbara's case, she might say to her class:

> **Try Saying This:**
>
> "Kids, I'm sorry that I overreacted to your noise level by shouting. I'm not feeling quite myself today. Let's start over."
>
> "I expect that you can make more of an effort to be quiet, and I'll make a better effort to let you know my expectations of you."

It's important to continuously take stock of your emotions and reactions when you lead children's groups. Don't judge yourself for becoming frustrated or upset with the kids. Instead, pay attention to your feelings. Self-awareness increases your consciousness. When you are conscious, you are able to communicate more clearly and effectively.

Victory Over Shyness
Helping the Introverted Child

Kristina is a very quiet, reserved eleven-year-old. She performs very well academically, but maintains her distance from the other kids at school. Rarely socializing outside of school, Kristina is comfortable only with her oldest and dearest friends. With these girls, Kristina is uncharacteristically chatty and carefree. Her shyness is especially profound in new situations when she's around unfamiliar kids or adults. In groups, Kristina remains on the sidelines, unable to join in. When her parents try to help her overcome her shyness by pressuring her into social situations, she resists.

A P.E. teacher once assigned Kristina to be a team captain in an effort to improve her leadership skills and combat her social isolation. But, Kristina didn't know the rules of the game and was quickly deemed incompetent by her classmates. Remanded to the sidelines, she was ignored by her teammates for the rest of the class. Kristina was humiliated and pretended to be sick the next day to avoid school. She returned to school the following week, but she couldn't stop thinking about the embarrassing events from her last P.E. class. She became even more withdrawn from her peers.

Shy children are terribly afraid of embarrassment. Extreme self-consciousness leads them to believe that others are judging them. Rather than risk embarrassment, shy children may avoid social situations. Their reluctance to seek out other kids can be read by their peers as odd or snobbish. On the contrary, shy kids typically like to be sought out. After some necessary warm-up time, they can play nicely and interact well with others.

You will recognize a shy child because she avoids initiating conversation, has trouble with direct eye contact, and may speak softly. The shy child will be the one who always sits in the back of the room and appears to be on the fringes of the group. She may eat alone in the cafeteria or hang back at team meetings.

Groups tend to make shy kids even more anxious. Navigating one-on-one interaction is difficult enough for the shy child without the additional complicated dimension of group dynamics. Consequently, shy kids tend to avoid social groups.

Unfortunately, the longer social situations are avoided, the harder it is for these kids to develop necessary social skills. As their social aptitude diminishes from lack of experience, the likelihood of social rejection increases, thus creating a vicious cycle where shyness and social anxiety is perpetuated. If left unaddressed, severe shyness can develop into full-blown social phobia, a morbid fear of social situations.

Groups offer an ideal place for children to learn social skills and to make friends. Friendship promotes the development of perspective taking and positive self-esteem. Kids like Kristina who place themselves on the periphery of the group miss out on the wonderful benefits a group provides for building friendships.

You have a wonderful opportunity as a group leader to help a socially withdrawn child improve and develop social skills. Shyness is best overcome through gentle exposure and practice. Although Kristina's P.E. teacher had good intentions, assigning her to be team captain was too much, too soon. You can't throw a child into the deep end of a pool and tell her to swim without first teaching her how to doggie paddle. Kristina was unprepared for the deep end! It's imperative to aid shy kids in learning the social steps they can take to improve their interactions. As important as it is to encourage shy children to socialize, make sure you do it slowly.

Joining In

Joining a group is not easy for most kids. It's especially challenging for shy children who may be overwhelmed by the interactions in a group setting. They have trouble "seeing the trees for the forest." For shy kids, you have to help them learn simple techniques for joining in.

① Practice finding the friendly face.

For Kristina, and many shy children, sizing up a large group of kids feels overwhelming. She just can't break down a group into smaller, more manageable parts. When she tries to join a mass of kids, she freezes with anxiety. But, if Kristina is taught how to search for the one or two kids who smile and appear approachable, she will have an easier time joining the group at her own pace.

I suggest you practice watching other kids at play with the shy child. Encourage her to pick out the kids who appear more open and friendly – the ones the shy child will have an easier time approaching. It is often the case that the children on the periphery of a group are friendlier. Kids who are the leaders of a group may not necessarily be the most welcoming.

② Rehearse what to say ahead of time.

Practice joining-in questions with the shy child. For instance, "Can I join?" or "Do you want to play?"

The shy child may not want to say anything when she joins in. Instead, she may be more comfortable going with the flow of the group without saying a word. This is fine. For example, if your group is playing tag, the shy child simply begins running from the person who is "it." She only needs to make sure to follow the rules of the game and just go with the flow to join in appropriately.

It's not really necessary for a child to introduce herself when joining a group. This actually may interrupt the flow of things. Names can be exchanged later after the group gets to know each other a bit through the games they're playing. Kids who have good social skills intuitively know how to join in unobtrusively.

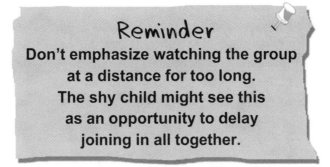

Reminder
**Don't emphasize watching the group
at a distance for too long.
The shy child might see this
as an opportunity to delay
joining in all together.**

The kids in your group who are impulsive by nature may need to watch the group interaction for a while before thoughtfully joining in. The shy child is not impulsive, but rather self-conscious. These kids watch themselves so carefully that they feel incapable of making any move at all! They worry that anything they say or do will be judged by their peers.

③ Role-play joining in.

Role-playing allows kids to practice skills before they need to use them in real-life situations. While you role-play, be sure to focus on potentially troublesome social scenarios and offer solutions to the problems.

Here's how to role-play:

> ▶ **Discuss the skill to be practiced.** Talk with the shy child about the skill you'll be working on. You may actually want to work on joining-in skills with *all* of the group members, especially if there is more than one shy child in the group. Role-play is a

terrific technique for getting everyone involved without singling out a specific person.

▶ **Rehearse the steps.** Verbally rehearse the steps necessary to master the skill. For joining in, you'll want to review the steps necessary to achieve that goal:

- Wait. Watch. Listen.
- Find the friendly face.
- Figure out what to say ahead of time. Actually come up with the line that will be used for joining in. For example, "Can I join in?"

▶ **Set the stage.** Create the scene where the skill is going to be used. For instance, if Kristina is having trouble joining a game at recess, the role-play can take place at recess. Pretend there is a group of kids playing a game that a child wants to join. When you role-play, the stage will be set for the action to take place.

▶ **Model the skill.** Show the kids exactly what they need to do to join in appropriately. It never hurts for the whole group to practice this skill, even if they are already pretty accomplished at it. You may want to play the role of a shy child at recess. (No one has to know that you are thinking of a specific child when you do the role-play.) Say out loud what you are thinking when you approach a group.

Try Thinking Aloud Like This:

"Hmm, I see that the other kids are playing tag."

"I see that Keisha is 'it' and all of the kids are running away from her."

"I'd like to play but I don't know what I would say. Maybe I could just run away from Amanda like everyone else. I'll go with the flow."

▶ **Have the kids practice the skill.** It's important that your group knows all the social steps before role-playing. You may need to review the sequence or even write it down. Also review the roles of all the "players." For instance, if another child is going to play a "friendly person" at the playground, review how she will respond. If you are going to play a "rejecting child," review ahead of time how the "joining-in child" will respond. Practice the skills, gradually increasing the degree of difficulty. Initially, the group of kids the joining-in child approaches can be accepting. Later, the group can role-play becoming more challenging to join, perhaps even rejecting. Practice with your kids different ways to handle rejection – perhaps the joiner just walks away and finds another group to play with, or perhaps she says to herself, "Oh well, maybe next time."

▶ **Practice role reversal.** In this exercise, you freeze the action in the middle of a role-play and allow the kids to take on the role of "the other." I have found this method very effective for kids who have a hard time seeing how their behavior affects others. When they are given the chance to view themselves through the eyes of the other, the experience can be eye-opening for them.

▶ **Give positive feedback.** Positive feedback is an excellent way to reinforce skills. Feedback can take the form of suggestions, coaching, praise, or support.

Encouraging the Shy Child

Having a shy temperament is not necessarily a bad thing. Some kids are naturally slower to warm up than others. Being shy only becomes problematic when the child's feelings of inhibition interfere with day-to-day activities. Consider the following when working with a shy child:

① **Maintain realistic expectations.**

Encourage the child to go with the flow of the group. At the same time, communicate that you understand her emotional experience. You can acknowledge her conflict between wanting to belong and fearing rejection, and still expect her to participate in the group. Participation does not necessarily mean verbal participation right away. If a shy child is engaged and smiling, but not yet ready to talk in the group, that's okay.

In our social skills training groups at *In Step*, there are some kids who do not participate verbally for several months. We can see that the child is listening and engaged, but not yet ready to speak. This does not stop us from addressing the reticent child and giving her opportunities to speak. Initially we may ask simple "yes" or "no" questions to help her warm up. And, slowly, as we persist, the shy child begins to speak more frequently. We don't give up. And neither should you!

Reminder

Continue to expect success from the shy child. Avoid the temptation to stop calling on her just because you sense her discomfort. Continue to call on every member of your group equally.

2 Help the child set realistic goals and a means to accomplish them.

During a quiet time, when you are alone with the shy child, let her know that you can see how difficult it is for her to speak in the group. Ask her if she would like help on becoming more verbal in the group. Reassure her that she can achieve her own goals at her own pace. Help her choose a goal that is attainable to avoid discouragement. Track progress toward the goal, and reward improvement with praise or a small reward, e.g., a sticker, a star, or an ice cream cone.

Sample Goals for the Shy Child

- ◗ Kristina will say "hello" to a group member each meeting.

- ◗ Kristina will join in to a group activity without being asked one time this week.

- ◗ Kristina will make one comment in the group without being asked.

- ◗ Kristina will sit next to a friendly child in the group today.

 Encourage positive self-talk.

Challenge the shy child's tendency to attribute negative thoughts and feelings to others. This negative self-talk only furthers feelings of hopelessness and loneliness in the shy child. Help her develop constructive alternatives to negative thinking.

Try Saying This:	Rather Than This:
"I have no evidence that this girl doesn't like me. I'm going to assume she likes me and treat her as such."	"That girl hates me."
"Maybe she is in a bad mood and this has nothing to do with me."	"That girl is mean to me so she hates me."
"I can say a lot with my eyes and my smile until I'm ready to say something."	"I have nothing to say."
"I am a very good student and have many interests to share."	"I am so stupid and boring."

④ Avoid negative labels and pressures to socially perform.

A child who is labeled and pressured is a child who feels backed into a corner. This will only serve to increase anxiety and result in more withdrawal. Go slowly. Be supportive.

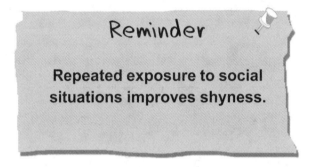

Reminder

Repeated exposure to social situations improves shyness.

Kids are able over time to lessen the anxiety that fuels shyness. Through repeated exposure to unfamiliar people and events, goal setting, and practice, social success is likely. However, as a group leader, be on the lookout for warning signs that a child's shyness is actually social anxiety. If the shy child in your group never warms up and continues to maintain minimal interaction with peers, it may be time for you to suggest professional counseling to her parents.

Wrestling with Boredom
Inspiring Motivation in Your Group

Tara has been coaching high school field hockey for years and she loves it. She enjoys watching the girls improve their skills over the course of a season. She especially loves the thrill of competition. Over the last few years, however, Tara has noticed that she is not having as much fun coaching as she did in the past. Every year the girls seem less and less engaged in the sport. Many of her girls convey an attitude of boredom and lack of motivation that inhibits their ability to enjoy the game. And their apathy is spreading to the other girls in the group, who don't want to be seen as enthusiastic when the established tone in the group is that of negativity and ennui. Tara recognizes a downward spiral when she sees one. She played on a team once when she was younger that had a similar dynamic. Her teammates weren't "into it." There is no way she is going to allow that to happen to this team! Tara is confident that she can find ways to help motivate the girls to motivate each other, before it's too late.

Kids! What's the matter with kids today? One of our biggest challenges in leading groups of children is keeping them motivated and engaged. Does this sound familiar? "I'm bored." "Who cares?" "Why do we have to do this anyway?" "This is stupid." Sometimes keeping kids charged-up can feel like pumping air into a balloon with a hole in it. Let's look at some of the reasons for this type of negativity we witness in groups.

Maintaining a Mask of Boredom

Teenagers, in particular, are masters at feigning indifference. I use the word "feigning" because the emotions these kids present to the outside world as defiance, avoidance, passivity, and even contempt do not accurately reflect how they feel on the inside. As teenagers' feelings swirl around inside of them, they put on outer masks of boredom and apathy to protect themselves. Teenagers are in flux. They are trying to understand themselves and to develop identities that are unique and different from the adults around them.

Sometimes, kids who are struggling with identity issues have no other choice but to define themselves in contrast to something or someone else. You, as the adult leader, are an ideal candidate to play this role.

Fear of Connection and Being Hurt

Other kids remain detached from you and the group because of a basic lack of trust in others. Children who have experienced emotional hurts and abuses may maintain an air of indifference to fend off connection for fear of being hurt again.

Virtual Passivity

Adults today frequently wonder why kids seem so utterly unable to entertain themselves. It's not that the children of this generation own the patent on boredom! I remember plenty of rainy days when I complained to my mother about being bored. But children today take boredom to a whole new level. They are virtually flooded with video games, high-tech gadgets, and other highly stimulating forms of passive entertainment that require very little of their imaginations. Thus, immediate gratification is at their fingertips. Kids get minimal practice at tapping into their own powers of resourcefulness. After all, resourcefulness is an ability to look within one's self to accomplish a task with the few tools that are available. We provide our kids with tons of tools, toys, and technology! Who needs resourcefulness? Unfortunately, when children are unable to motivate and entertain themselves, they look to us to fix it when then their toys aren't available to them.

Poor Self-Confidence and Fear of Making Mistakes

This may seem like a paradox, but some kids so strongly need to do every task perfectly, without error, that they are frozen in a state of inaction. If they don't try, then they can't fail. These children say to themselves, "If I had tried, I would have succeeded. I just didn't try." These kids may feel that they have no value without performing to the unreasonable level of this self-imposed standard.

"Boring" and "Stupid"— Code for Internal Emptiness

The words "boring" and "stupid" are without a doubt the most common descriptors used by unmotivated kids. Everything is boring and stupid. School is boring. Family is stupid. The group is boring *and* stupid. The child's use of these words to describe his external world is really a reflection of the emptiness of his internal world. These kids believe that joy and entertainment come from the outside in, rather than the other way around. They have trouble seeing that their own actions, commitment, and engagement is connected to their experience in a group.

You've become a group leader because you enjoy kids and you want to create a group that is fun and productive. At the same time, we know that for groups to be successful, the kids themselves have to help create the tone and climate of the group. Kids and adults alike learn best when they have bought in to the process of the group. Ideally, each member of your group wants to be there and has a goal he is working toward. It's your job as the leader to capitalize on the kids' intrinsic motivations for being there.

Here are some steps you can take to inspire motivation in your group:

 ## Use humor to diffuse tension.

I asked my two teenage sons recently, "What's the most effective way your teachers or coaches have handled Attitudes (with a capital "A") on the part of their kids?" Simultaneously, without skipping a beat, they answered, "With humor!" They both agreed that leaders who take themselves or kids' attitudes too seriously have little chance of turning the bored kids around to become motivated and productive group members.

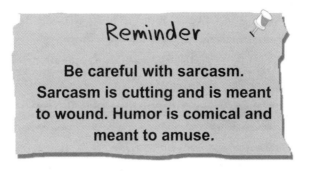

Reminder

Be careful with sarcasm. Sarcasm is cutting and is meant to wound. Humor is comical and meant to amuse.

(2) Get kids to use their heads.

It's easy to get into the habit of telling your group members what to do. "Open your books to page…." "Pass the ball!" "Lights out in 10 minutes." "Let me tell you how I want this done." Kids are so used to adults droning on and on about subjects they have no interest in that they have been conditioned to tune us out. Good leaders look for opportunities to ask questions of their group members whenever possible. Asking questions helps the kids feel involved and that their opinions matter.

"Where are you going if the ball is hit over Isaac's head?"

"What are we working on today?"

"What did you see Regina do that made that play work well?"

"Who can explain this concept to the group? I bet one of you can say it more clearly than me."

"That didn't work out quite the way you wanted. Nice try. What did you learn from it?"

③ Have the kids teach each other.

You can incorporate team teaching exercises into your everyday routine. After you've taught the kids a new concept, ask one of the kids to demonstrate the skill for the rest of the group. Then, break the kids into small groups to practice their newly learned skill in front of each other. Feedback after each demonstration is important. Encourage the group to focus on what their fellow group members did right and say it out loud.

Reminder

Kids are going to be more inspired by feedback from their peers than by feedback from you.

4 Have the kids come up with their own goals for their group participation.

Resist the urge to suggest goals for each of the kids. Let them struggle a little to come up with their own answers to these questions: "Why are you here?" "What do you want to get out of this group?" Help the kids be as specific as possible in their goal setting. "I want to become a better player" or "I want to make a friend" are nice goals, but they're too vague and hard to track. Instead, encourage the kids to come up with measurable goals like, "I want to be able to make 40% of my free throws" or "I want to get together socially with one group member before our next meeting."

More passive kids will have a difficult time coming up with their own goals. They would just as soon have you tell them what to do so they don't have to think about it themselves. In this case, it's okay for you to suggest a couple of specific goals and ask the child to choose which of the goals makes sense to him personally. Even better, ask the rest of the group to come up with a plausible goal for the resistant child. This is when peer pressure is used to your advantage!

In our teenage groups, in particular, the phenomenon of the passive-resistant group member is common. Frequently, these teens will say that the only reason they're in a therapy group is because "my parents made me join." This may be an answer to the question, "Why are you in this group?" but it does not answer the question, "What would you like to achieve in this group?" or "How can you get what you need out of this group?" When the majority of kids answer the above questions honestly and openly by setting group goals for themselves, they set the stage for the passive-resistant group members to follow suit and take responsibility for their own group experiences.

Reminder

Make sure you write down the goals and check back with each child regarding progress on a regular basis. When you do this, you communicate to your kids that you are interested and invested in their success.

5 Focus on the process rather than the outcome.

In our goal-oriented society, kids are frequently praised only after completion of a goal. Any goal that is worth achieving requires effort. When you praise the process of getting there, rather than the outcome, you help keep the momentum moving forward and the kids engaged. Children who are encouraged to focus only on the end result become discouraged, overwhelmed, and eventually shut down. When you highlight the connection between actions and outcome, you are helping the kids break down a goal into small, discrete steps that they can achieve and be proud of.

Try Saying This:

"I can see that you are really getting the hang of passing the ball."

"You are really sticking to your goal today!"

"You are working hard to stay focused during this activity."

6 Speak the language of the unmotivated.

Now that we understand that the attitudes of these children are often a reflection not of you or of your group, but of deep-seated feelings about the self, it's important not to let these kids push your buttons. If you become frustrated or destructive in your communication with these kids in the hopes of engaging them, you are actually just reinforcing their own negative perceptions of themselves. Instead, use the following constructive communication strategies.

Ask open-ended questions.

Kids who are shut down love "yes" or "no" questions. "Are you okay?"… "Yes." "Did you think about what we talked about last week in group?"… "Yes." "Do you need any help?" … "No." Closed-ended questions like the ones above limit communication, which is just what the apathetic child *wants* (but doesn't *need*).

When you ask open-ended questions instead, you demonstrate that you are really interested in what the child is feeling and thinking. "Tell me about the hardest part of our group today." "What things did you learn today in practice?" Open-ended questions lead to meaningful responses. They pave the road to engagement and involvement.

Identify aloud the feelings underneath the complaint.

We want our kids to enjoy and learn from our groups, so when they express themselves negatively, it's not hard to feel wounded. It's tempting to re-spond to your hurt feelings by denying the feelings of your unmotivated kids. Then, you may try (in vain) to get them to feel what you want them to feel. "You don't feel that way. Look at how great this group is!" Unfortu-nately, this method is ineffective, even destructive. It's okay for your kids to have negative feelings. It's your job to let them know that you understand their feelings and help lead them to make positive behavioral choices. This doesn't mean that you condone apathy in your group.

When Tara hears one of her girls complain of being bored, it's okay for her to say, "It seems like you are really bored in practice today. Tell me about an exercise we've played in the past that you *did* like, and we'll do it!" Tara can also engage the rest of the group to speak for her: "Hey, guys, what's an activity we've done in the past that has been challenging *and* fun? We need a picker-upper!"

Stay neutral.

Don't fall into the trap of believing that the only way to motivate the kids is to get angry and yell at them. This method may work in the short term – the kids will do what you say to avoid your anger. Unfortunately, it does nothing to help the kids develop their own internal motivation that can be maintained over time. It communicates the message, "I really don't have to do anything in this group *until* my group leader yells at me," rather than, "I need to figure out how to get what I need out of this group."

If you feel yourself getting frustrated, take a mental break before resuming interaction.

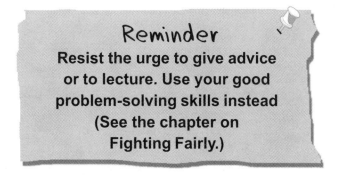

Reminder
Resist the urge to give advice or to lecture. Use your good problem-solving skills instead (See the chapter on Fighting Fairly.)

Encourage good questions.

It's critical that your group is a safe place for the kids to ask you questions. Questions are a way that your kids communicate that they are interested in what you or their fellow group members have to say. If you unintentionally communicate frustration or judgment when asked a question, the kids will stop asking. When they stop asking, they disengage. You want to prevent that from happening.

Adult Responses that Shut Kids Down

"Weren't you paying attention when I told you the first time?"

"You've never heard of a 'Renaissance Man'! Where have you been?"

"We've gone over this enough. Let's move on."

Adult Responses that Engage Kids

"That's a great question!"

"Very interesting question. Who can help me answer it?"

"Help me to understand what you are struggling with."

The best leaders are those who inspire their group members to learn. The goal is to help motivate the kids to make a consistent effort in your group. With positive support and encouragement, your kids will begin to take responsibility for their own experience in the group. When this happens, there is little room for boredom.

Xamine Your Zen
Finding Your Way

Your road to successful group leadership is paved with good intentions and a lot of hard work. Your job is one that is constantly evolving. Instead of focusing on some end point, you are learning and practicing new skills all the time to improve yourself as a leader of children. Strong leadership involves looking within to honestly appraise your own strengths and weaknesses as a leader, as well as looking outside of yourself to gauge how your kids interact with you and each other. There is a continuous synergy between these two processes. You check in on your own feelings and reactions to help you manage your actions in your group as you simultaneously observe the climate and interpersonal tenor of the group to help you alter your behavior as needed.

Remember that building your leadership strengths is no easy task. You may find that after reading this book, practicing the exercises recommended, and reviewing lessons learned that you still struggle to be the kind of leader you want to be with your kids. Don't be discouraged. It may take some time for you to get proficient at using the suggested strategies in this book. Initially, they may feel forced and unnatural. I assure you that if you act "as if" you are comfortable with the techniques (even before you actually *do* feel comfortable) the skills will soon become a seamless part of your leadership style. Like any new skill, practice is going to make all of the difference. I encourage you to go back over the chapters that were most challenging for you and spend as much time as you need to incorporate these techniques into your work with kids.

The best leaders continue to learn and grow right along with their groups. By trying to become a better leader, you are, by proxy, helping your group achieve its goals. Good luck, and keep up the good work!